Big and Small

To Parents: Pages 1 to 3 are used for learning opposite words. Have your child say "big" while pointing to the elephant and "small" while pointing to the mouse. Ask them what the opposite of "big" is.

Color the elephant's ears. Then put the mouse sticker on .

It's the opposite word!

Long and Short

To Parents: Have your child say "long" while pointing to the first dog and "short" while pointing to the second dog. Then say, "The body of the first dog became longer!" while closing and opening the page.

Fold and unfold the page, and say "long" and "short."

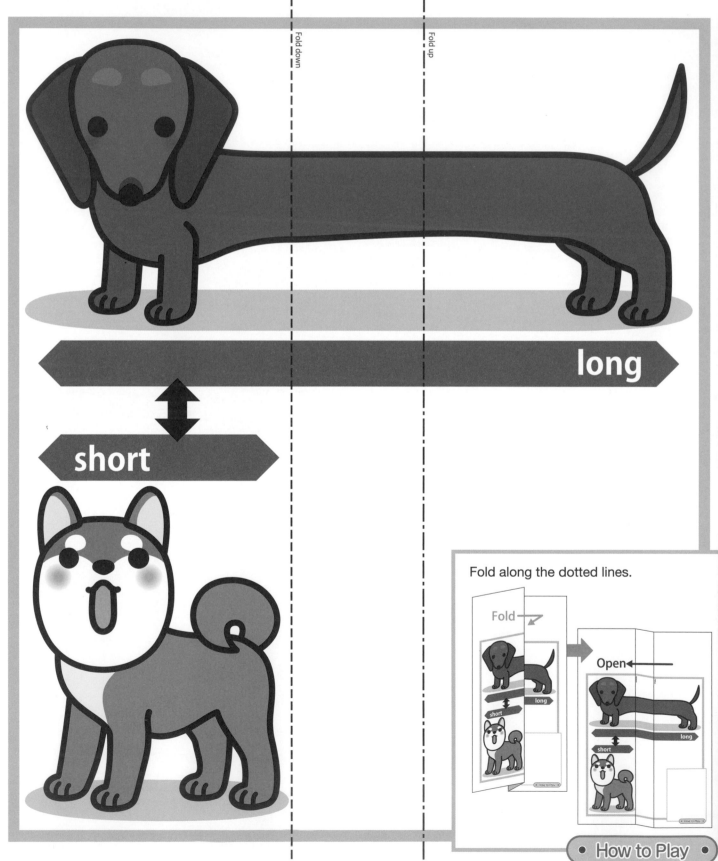

Fold down

Fold up

long

short

How to Play

Fold along the dotted lines.

Fold

Open

long

short

Slow and Fast

To Parents: Have your child say "slow" while pointing to the first rabbit and "fast" while pointing to the second rabbit. Then say, "The rabbit in the cart goes faster!" while closing and opening the page.

  Fold and unfold the page, and say "slow" and "fast."

Fold up

Fold down

How to Play

Fold along the dotted lines.

Fold

Open

slow

fast

Oh!

Draw Faces

To Parents: Encourage your child to draw smiling and angry faces on the soap bubbles below. Your involvement will keep them motivated!

Draw a face on each soap bubble.

example

Find the Same Shape

To Parents: Point out that the color of each shape matches its frame. When matching the pieces, say the name of each shape for your child: triangle, circle, and square.

Cut out the pieces at the bottom of the page. Then put each shape within its matching frame.

Cut out the shape.

How to Play

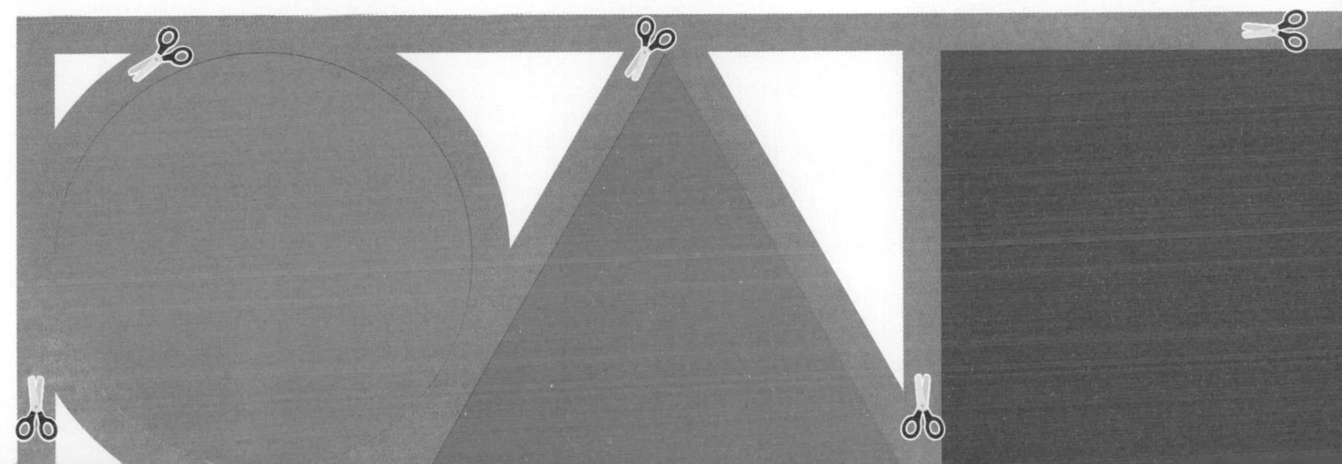

Find the Same Shape

To Parents: This activity focuses on recognizing colors and shapes. Help your child recognize the shapes by asking, "Which is a blue circle?" If it seems difficult for your child to draw a long, continuous line, have them stop once, and then continue drawing.

Draw a line to connect each shape on the left to the matching shape on the right.

example

heart

circle

Make Shape Cards

To Parents: In this activity, your child will improve memory.

Follow the instructions to make shape cards.

How to Make

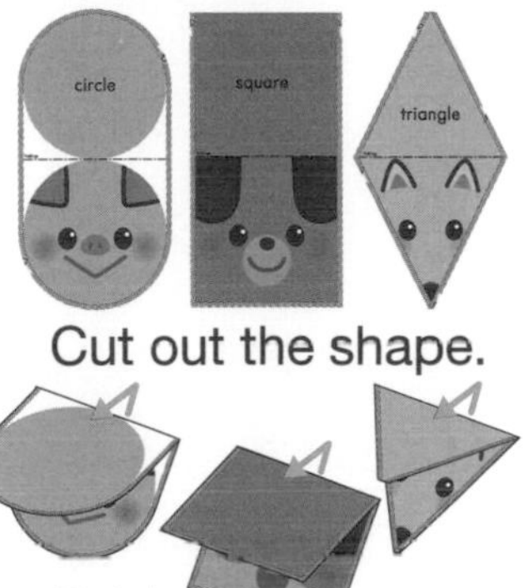

circle
square
triangle

Cut out the shape.

Fold

How to Play

What is this circle?

?

Close

pig!

Open

What is this circle?

pig!

That's right!

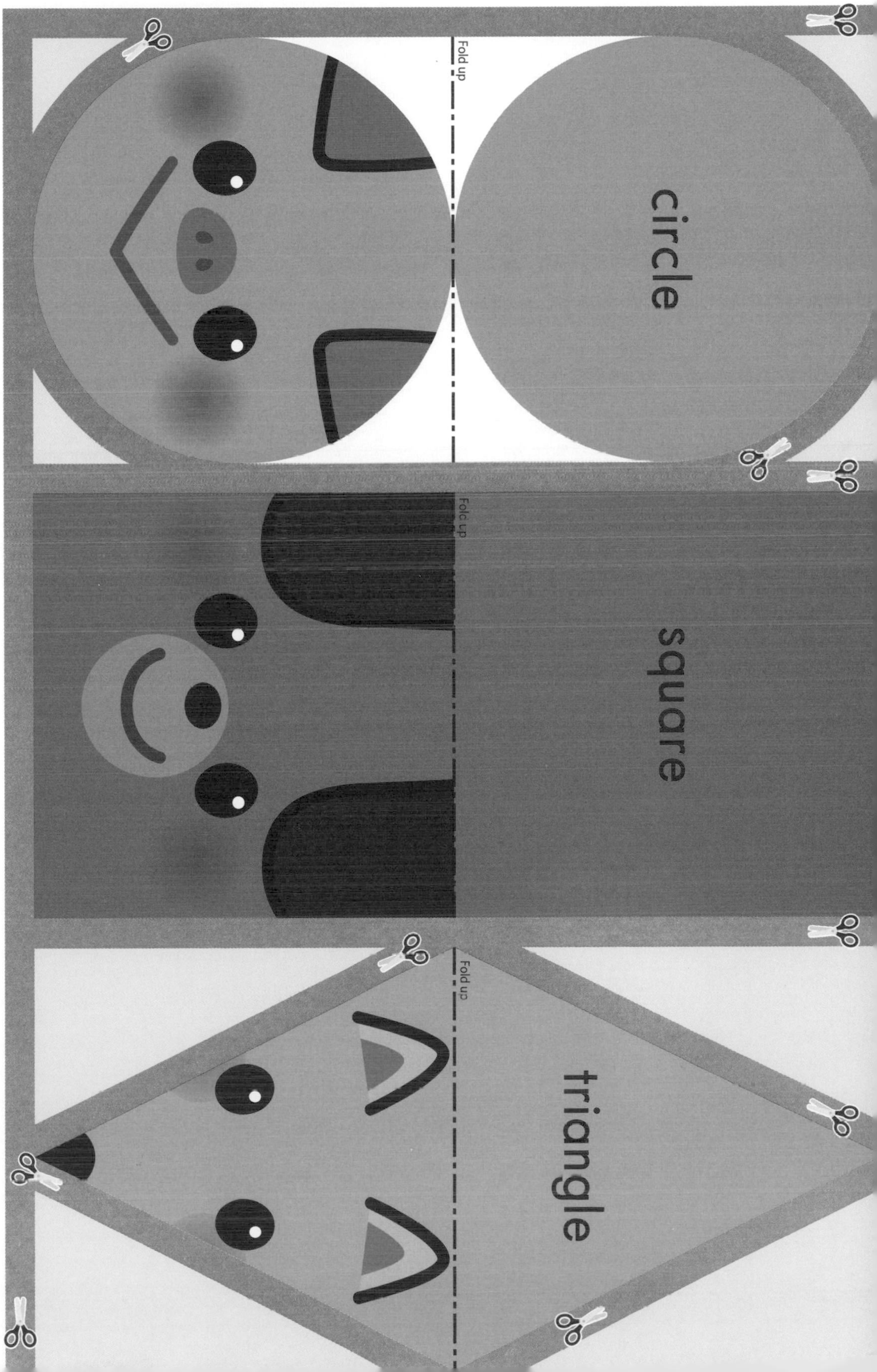

Fold up

circle

Fold up

square

Fold up

triangle

Make Shape Cards

To Parents: When done playing with the cards, switch roles between you and your child.

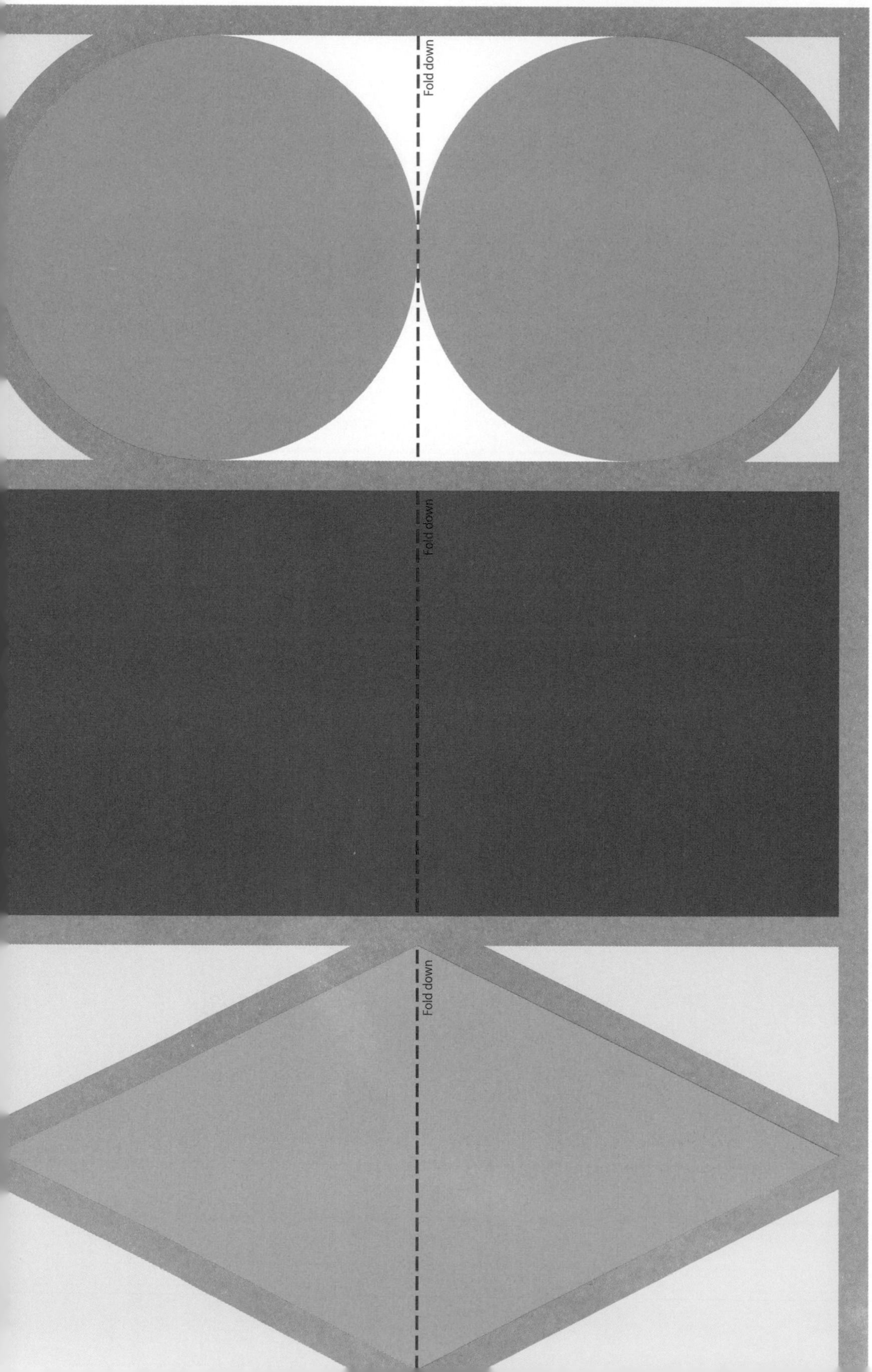

Fold down

Fold down

Fold down

pig

dog

fox

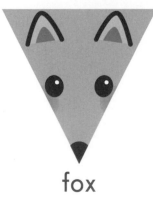

Picture Puzzles

To Parents: This activity helps develop spatial reasoning ability. Have your child focus on the shape of each puzzle piece. If this seems difficult, cut out the pieces after finishing the activity on the back of this page. Then ask your child which pieces fit together.

Draw lines to connect each matching vehicle.

example

Color the Shapes

To Parents: Ask your child to say the shape of each fish. If they forget the name of a shape, revisit pages 7 and 8. Then try again.

Color the fish with your favorite colors.

example

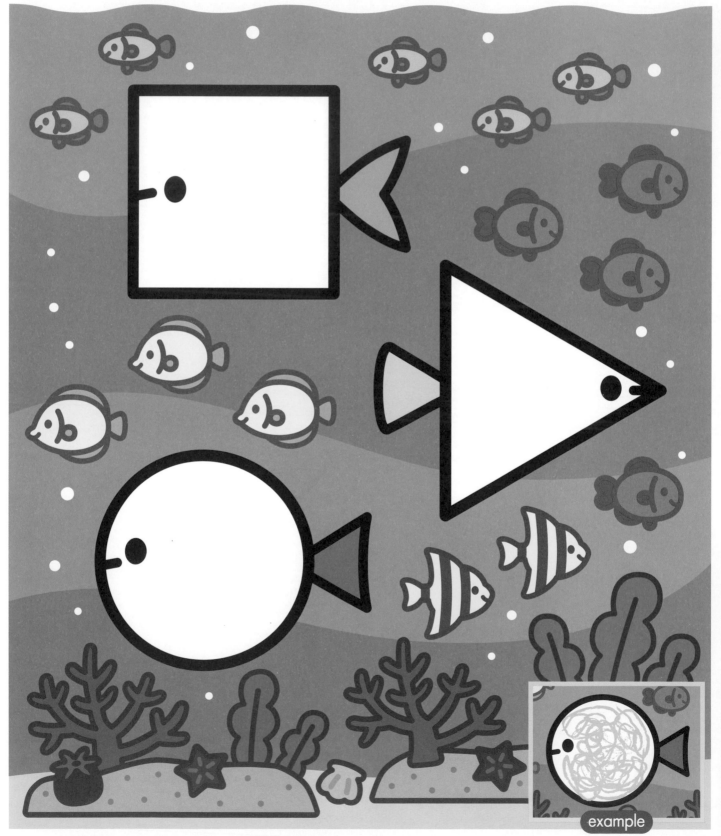

Bonus Challenge! Say the name of each shape.

Guess the Animals

To Parents: Give your child a clue by saying something like, "This animal's ears are long" or "It hops around." If this seems difficult, fold the page to confirm the answer. Then ask them to try again.

Name each animal's shadow.

How to Make

❶ Fold along the dotted lines.

❷ Cut along the gray lines.

How to Play

What animal's shadow is this?
Lion!
close
That's right!

Fold up

Fold up

Fold up

Fold up

Sticker
Good job!

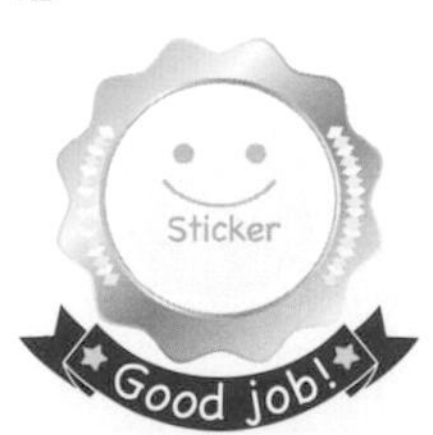

Trace Lines

To Parents: In this activity, your child will practice drawing wavy lines. If this seems difficult, put your hand on your child's to help them draw.

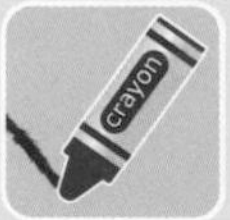

crayon
sticker

Fold down
lion
Fold down
giraffe
Fold down
rabbit
Fold down
dog

Trace lines from ➡ to ➡. Put stickers on .

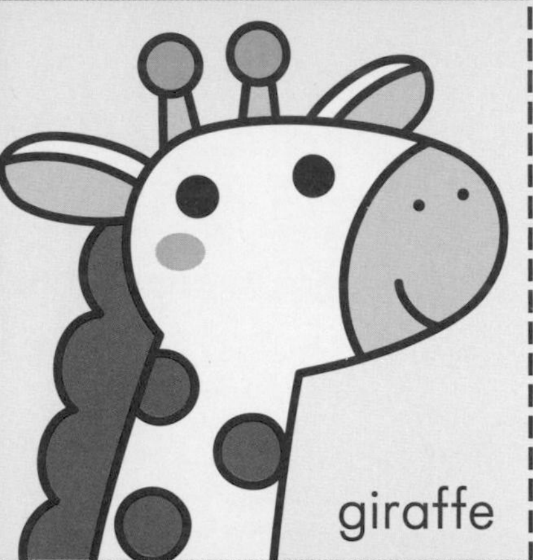

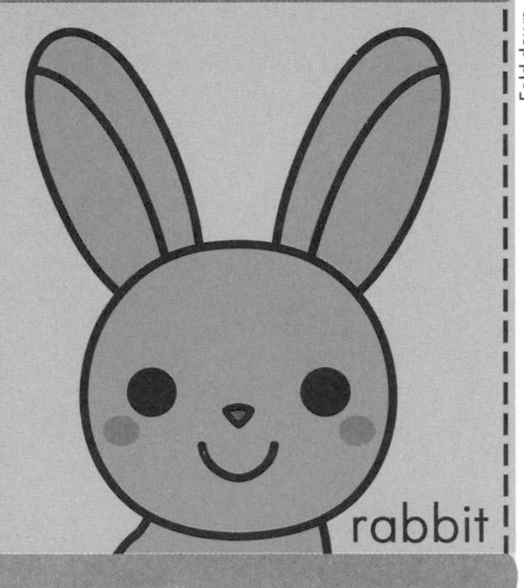

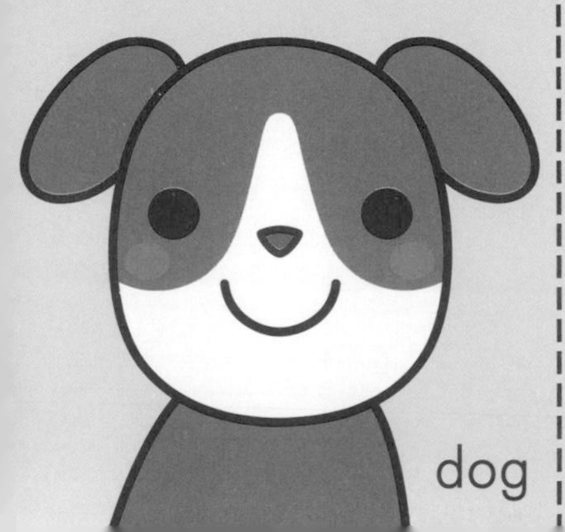

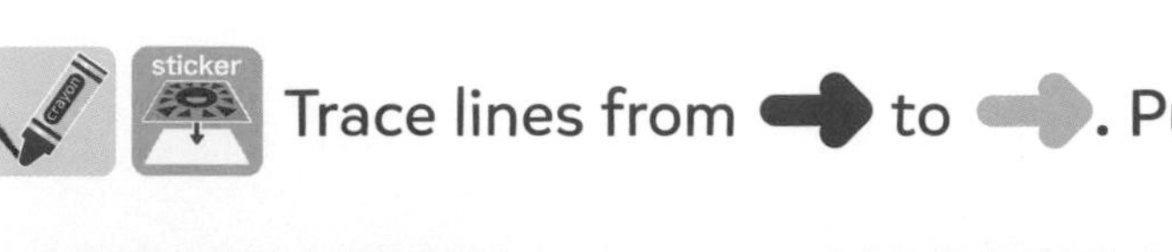

crayon
sticker
sticker

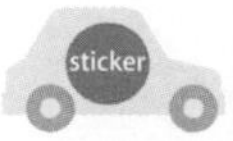

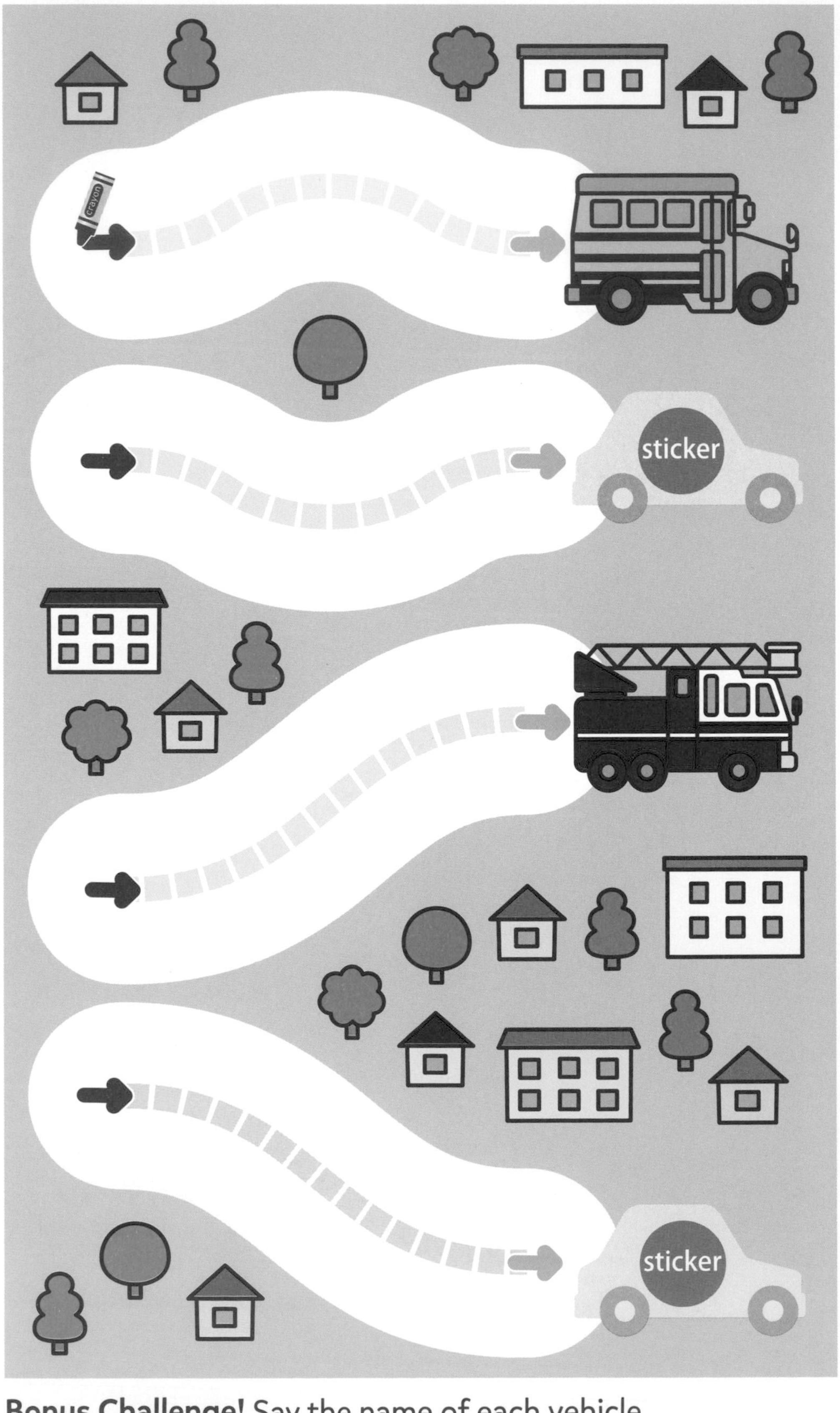

Bonus Challenge! Say the name of each vehicle.

Play with Cards

To Parents: The cards on pages 13, 15, and 17 are used for the "Two-Piece Puzzle" game. The cards on pages 14, 16, and 18 are used for the "Color Order" and "Color Match" games. To learn how to play the games, refer to pages 13, 15, and 20.

Sticker
Good job!

Play card games! Follow the instructions on pages 13, 15, and 17.

How to Make

Cut along the gray lines.

Which cards match to make one picture?

How to Play 1

Two-Piece Puzzle

Spread out the cards and find a pair to make a picture.

Start with a small number of cards to match and gradually increase the number of cards.

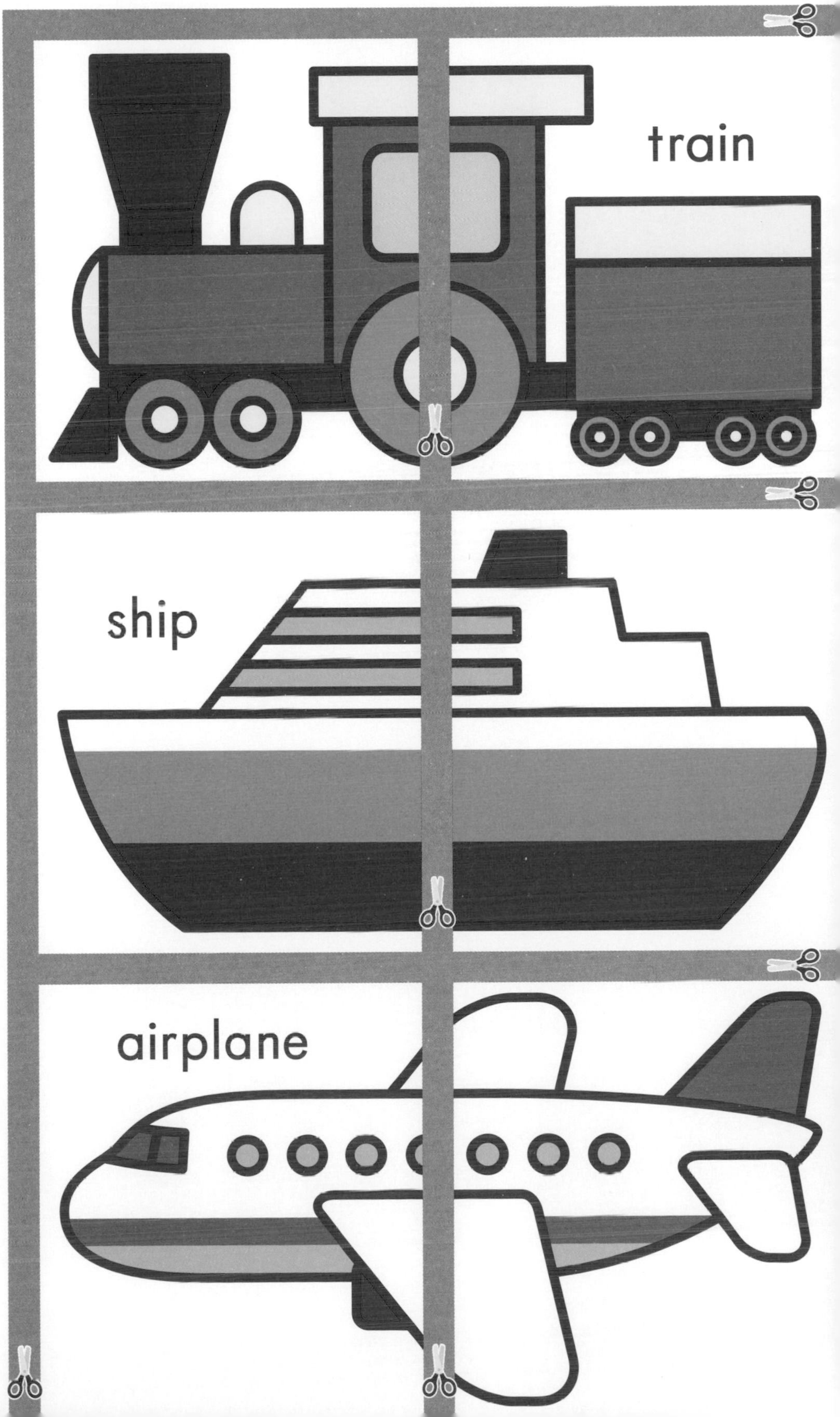

train

ship

airplane

Play with Cards

To Parents: Cut out the cards from pages 13 to 20.

Follow the instructions on page 20.

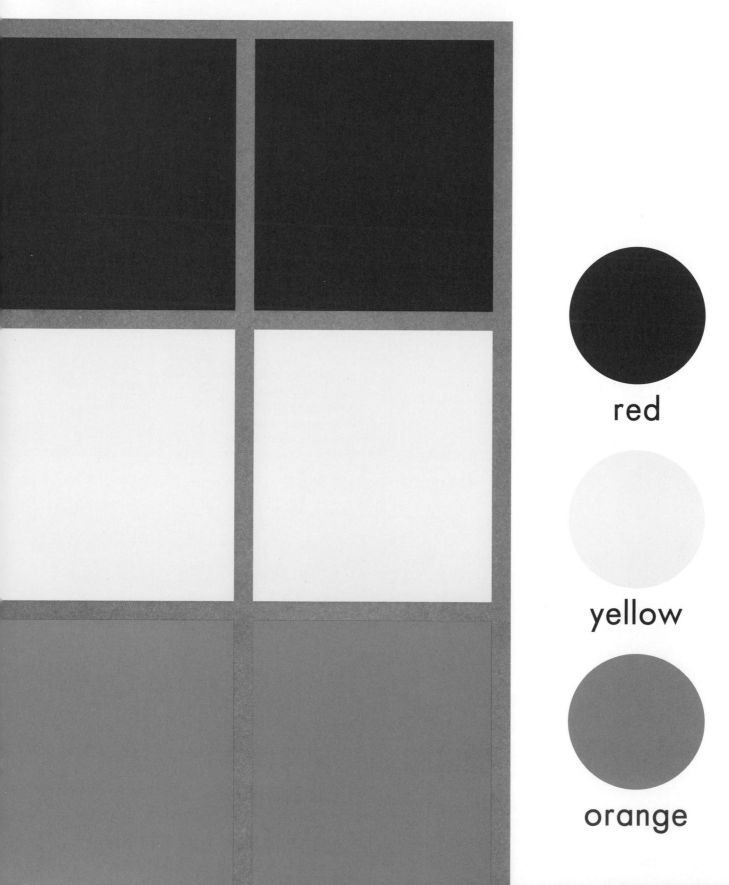

red

yellow

orange

Play with Cards

To Parents: Cut out the cards from pages 13 to 20.

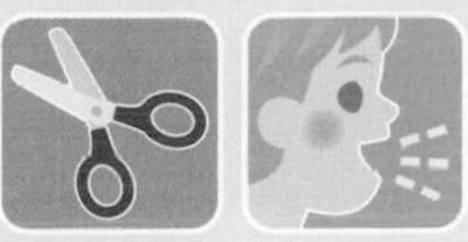

  Play card games! Follow the instructions on pages 13, 15, and 17.

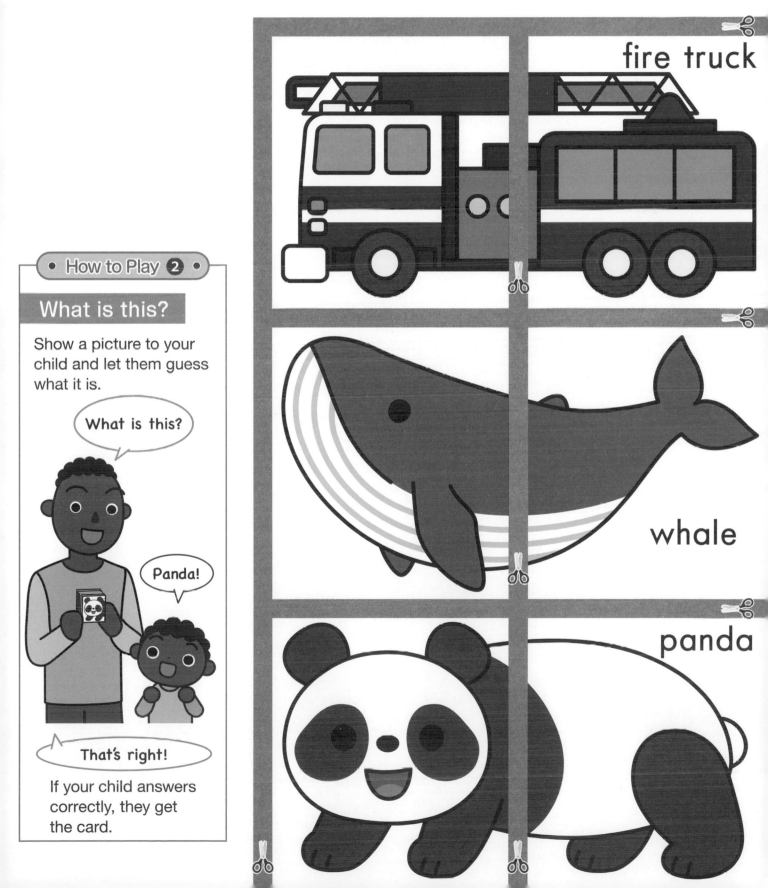

fire truck

whale

panda

• How to Play 2 •

What is this?

Show a picture to your child and let them guess what it is.

What is this?

Panda!

That's right!

If your child answers correctly, they get the card.

Play with Cards

To Parents: Cut out the cards from pages 13 to 20.

 Follow the instructions on page 20.

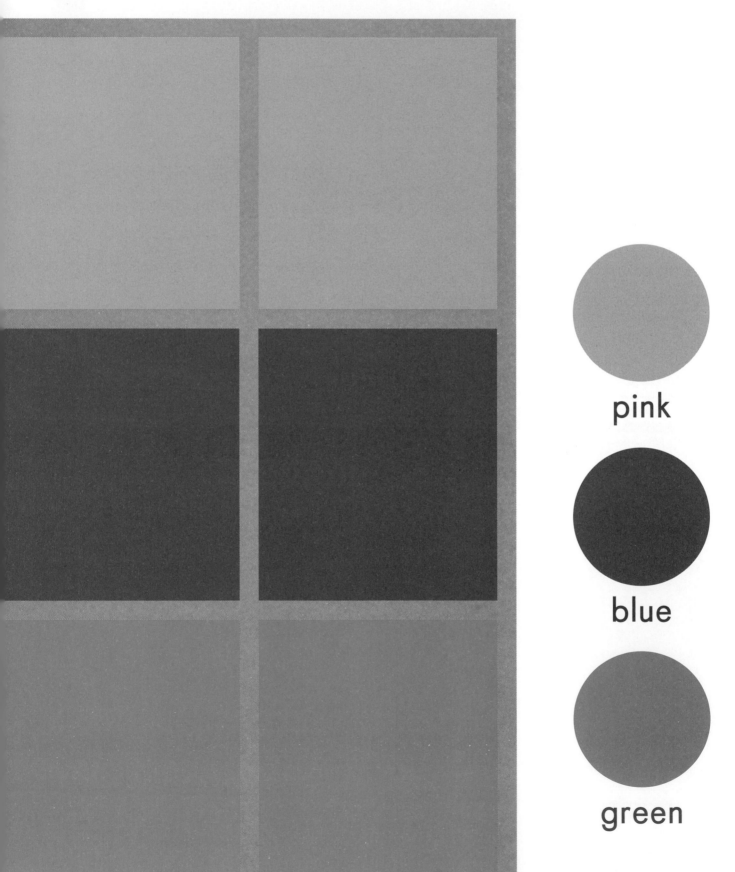

Play with Cards

To Parents: Cut out the cards from pages 13 to 20.

 Play card games! Follow the instructions on pages 13, 15, and 17.

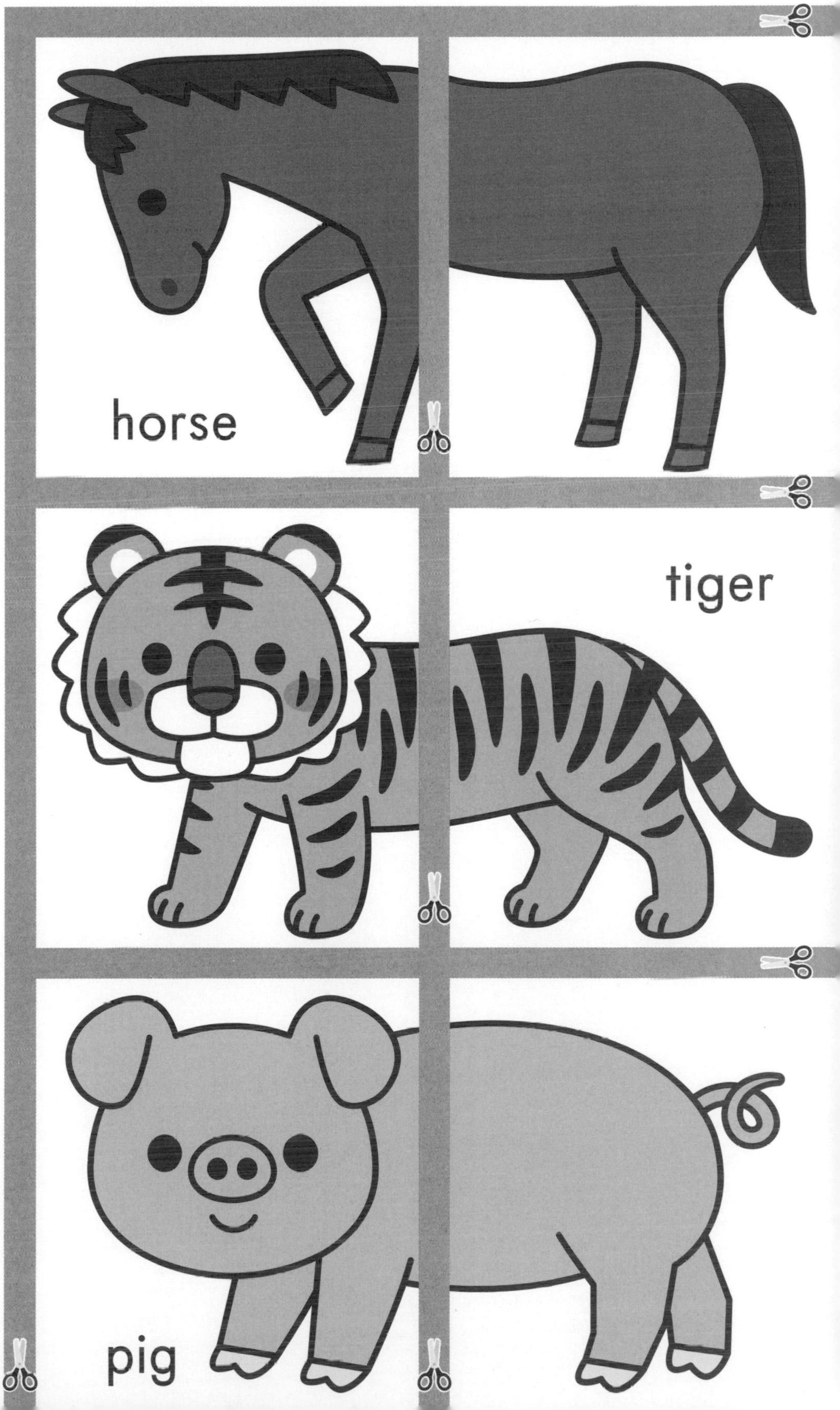

horse

tiger

pig

Play with Cards

To Parents: Cut out the cards from pages 13 to 20.

Follow the instructions on page 20.

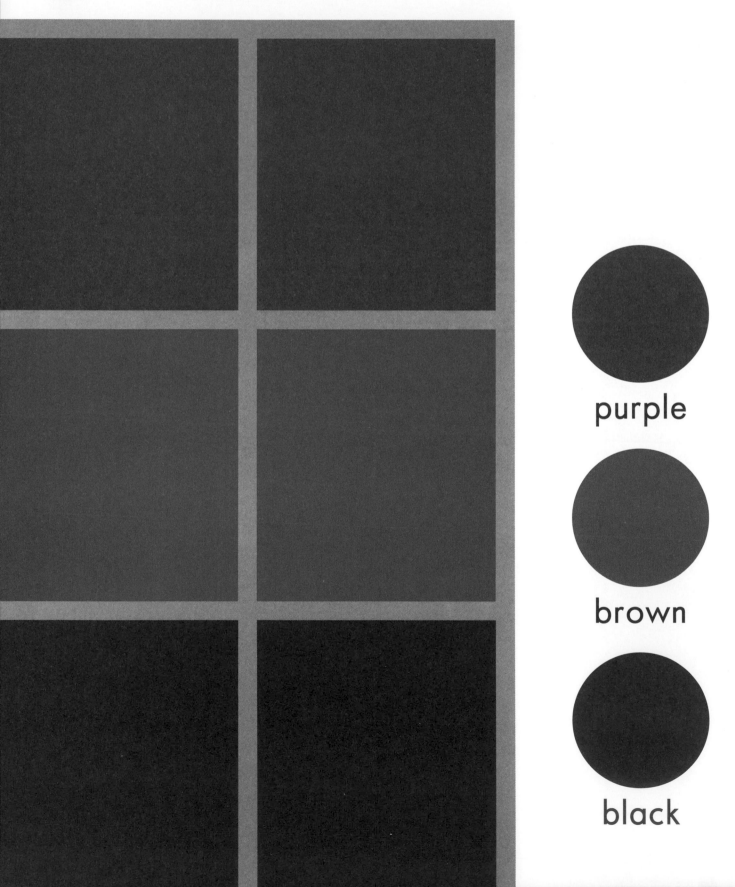

Play with Cards

To Parents: This activity creates a storing case for the cards on pages 13-18. When your child is done playing, ask them to put their cards in the case.

Follow the instructions to make the card case.

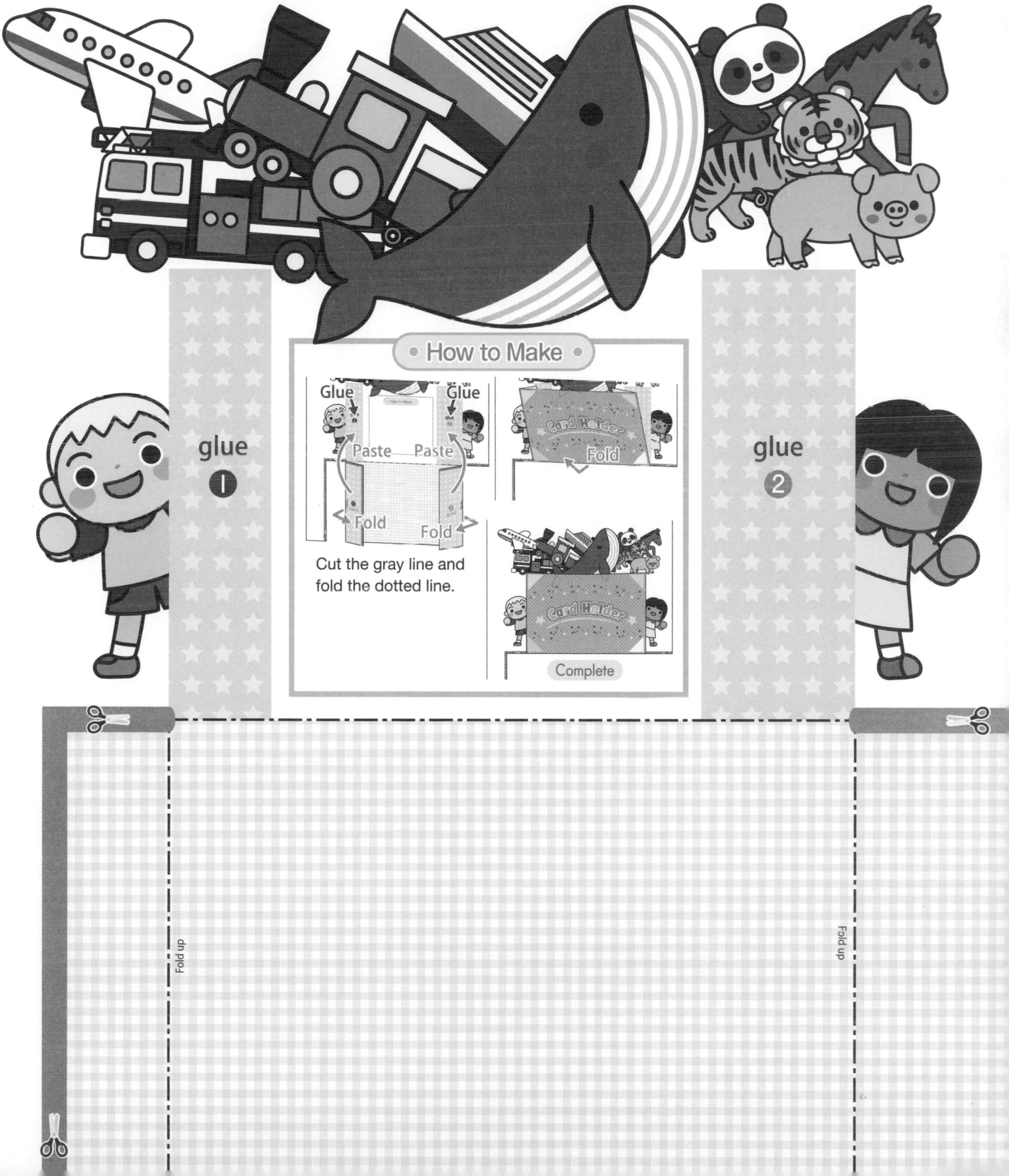

glue 1

glue 2

How to Make

Glue Glue

Paste Paste

Fold Fold

Cut the gray line and fold the dotted line.

Fold

Complete

Fold up

Fold up

Play with Color Cards

To Parents: In this activity, your child will practice memorizing the names of colors. In the Color Match Game, start with about six cards. Your child will be motivated to join the game by collecting matching cards.

How to Play Follow the instructions to play color card games.

Color Order Game

Place the color cards on a table. Have your child arrange the remaining color cards in the same order.

Color Match Game

Spread out the color cards on a table. Say the name of a color and have your child find the match.

Bonus Challenge! Arrange the cards in a row and say the name of each color in the order they appear.

Trace Lines

To Parents: In this activity, your child will practice drawing long and jagged lines. If this seems difficult, put your hand on your child's to help them draw.

Trace lines from  to . Put a sticker on .

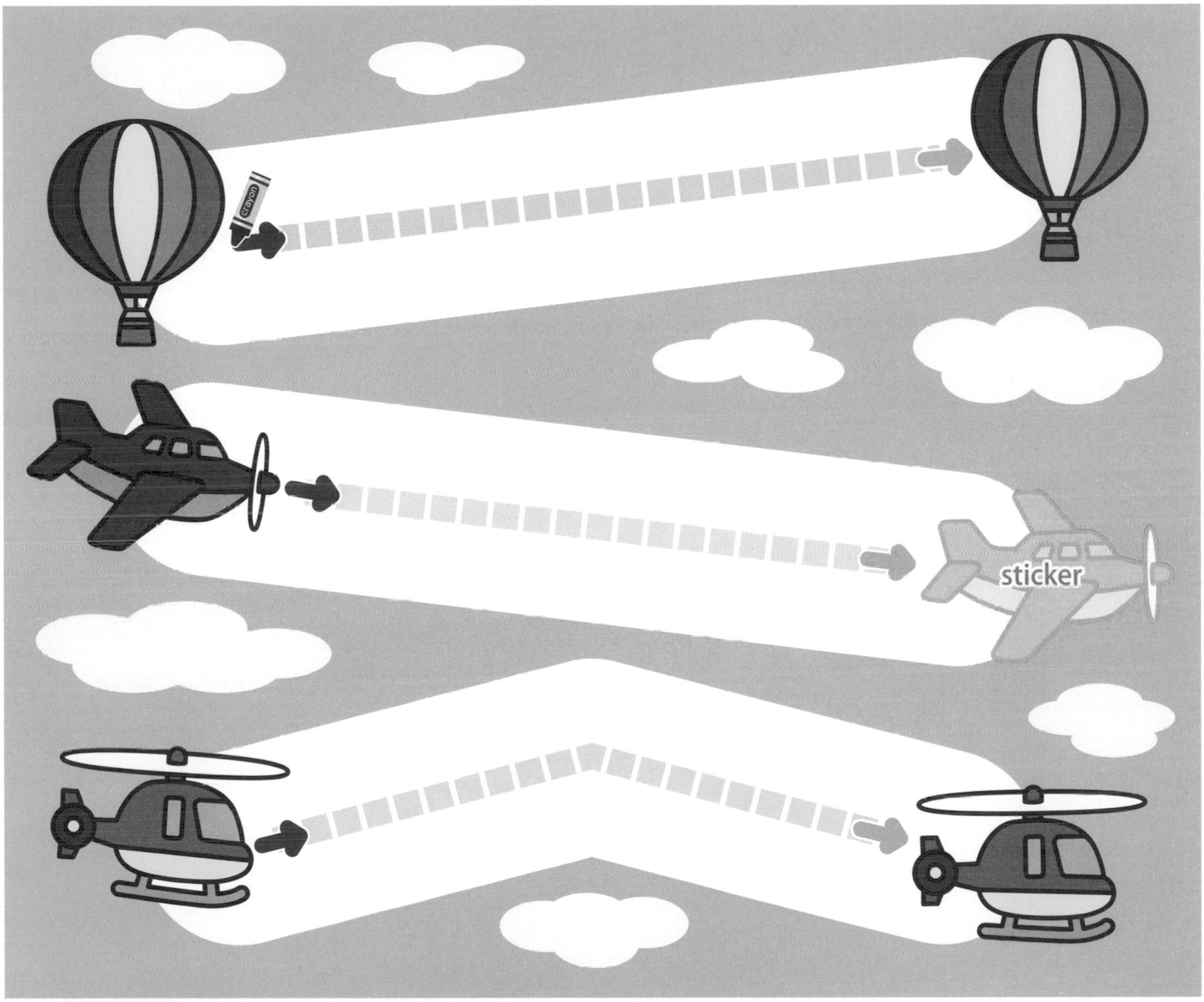

crayon

sticker

Bonus Challenge! Say the name of each vehicle.

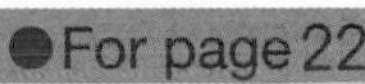
●For page 22

Make Bananas

To Parents: Encourage your child to tear the paper into various shapes of bananas. If this seems difficult, divide the larger piece of paper into two or three smaller pieces and have them tear those.

Cut out the yellow paper below. Tear it into banana shapes and glue them under the tree.

example

Bonus Challenge! Put the monkey stickers wherever you like.

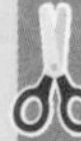

Color the Sea

To Parents: This activity focuses on creativity and handwriting. Have your child draw squiggles in the white space. It is okay if they color outside of this space.

Color the sea and put stickers on it.

example

Bonus Challenge! Put the starfish, shell, and crab stickers wherever you like.

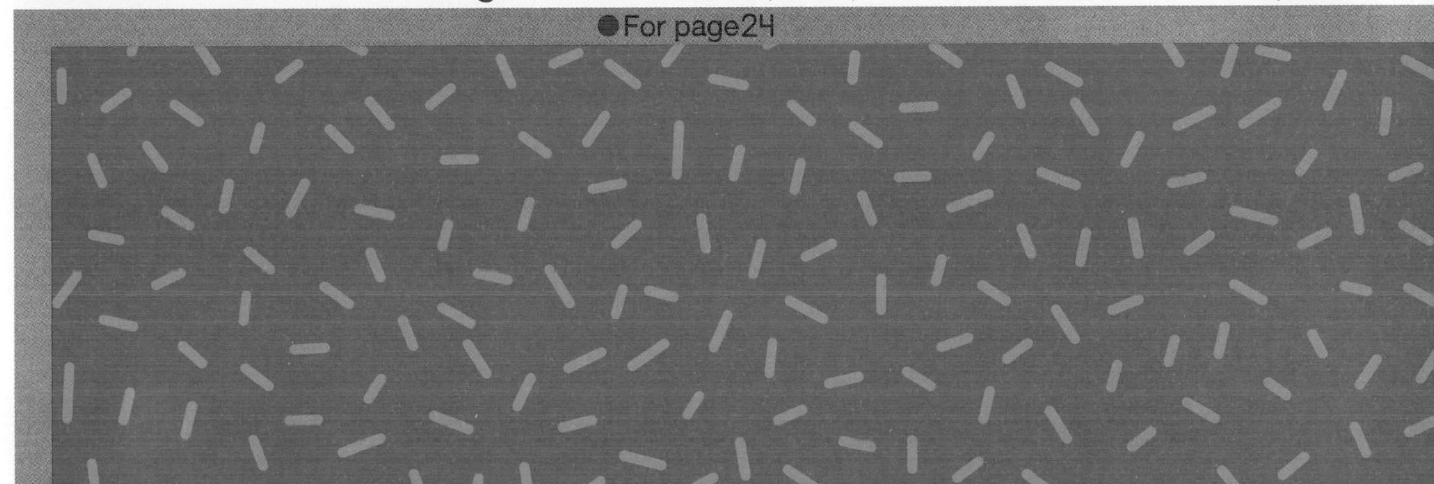

Make Cactuses

To Parents: Encourage your child to tear the paper into cactus shapes. If this seems difficult, divide the larger piece of paper into two or three smaller pieces and have them tear those. When done, praise your child by saying, "You made a great cactus!"

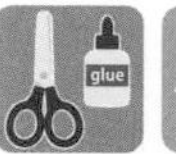

Cut out the green paper below. Tear it into cactus shapes and glue them on the desert.

example

Bonus Challenge! Put the lizard and the hedgehog stickers wherever you like.

Make Strawberries

To Parents: The front and back of the paper are different colors, so children can make different kinds of strawberries by folding the paper. If they are not yet used to gluing, have them put glue on just part of the strawberry.

Cut out the red paper below. Tear it into the shape of strawberries and glue them on the leaves.

How to Play

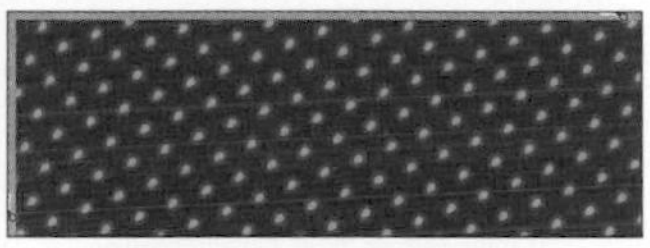

Cut the gray lines.

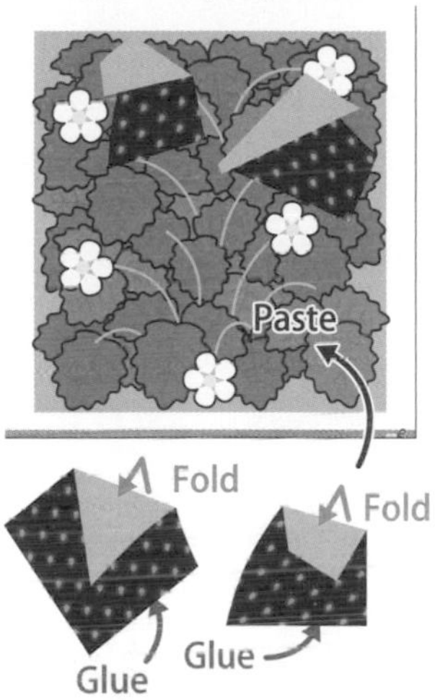

Paste

Fold

Fold

Glue

Glue

Tear the red paper and fold the top.

example

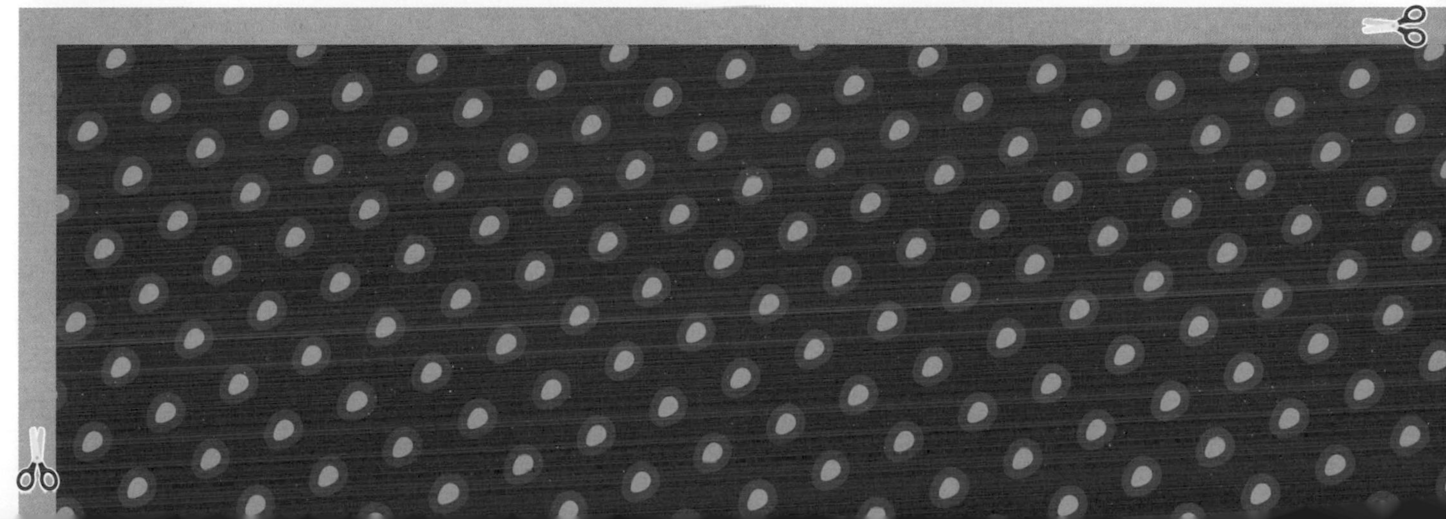

Find the Different Animal

To Parents: In this activity, your child will practice comparing different objects. Encourage them to pay attention to the colors.

One animal is different from the others. Find it and draw a ◯ around it.

Bonus Challenge! Find the penguin with a different facial expression.

Find the Same Food

To Parents: Ask your child the kinds of vegetables and fruits they've eaten. This helps them build their vocabulary based on what they know and their interests.

Draw a line from each fruit and vegetable in the ☐ to its match in the picture.

watermelon
apple
orange
corn
banana
potato
onion
avocado
tomato

example

banana
orange
tomato
lettuce
potato

Bonus Challenge! Find the red food and say its name.

Which Is More?

To Parents: Have your child practice finding "less or more" visually without counting the things. Ask which plate looks like it has more on it. One clue you can give is that the bigger portion covers up more of the plate!

Which plate has more jelly beans? Put a  sticker on the plate that has more jelly beans on it.

Which plate has more cookies? Put a  sticker on the plate that has more cookies on it.

Which Is Longer?

To Parents: Give your child a hint by telling them that the green plates are the same size.

Which sandwich is longer? Put a  sticker on the plate that has the longer sandwich on it.

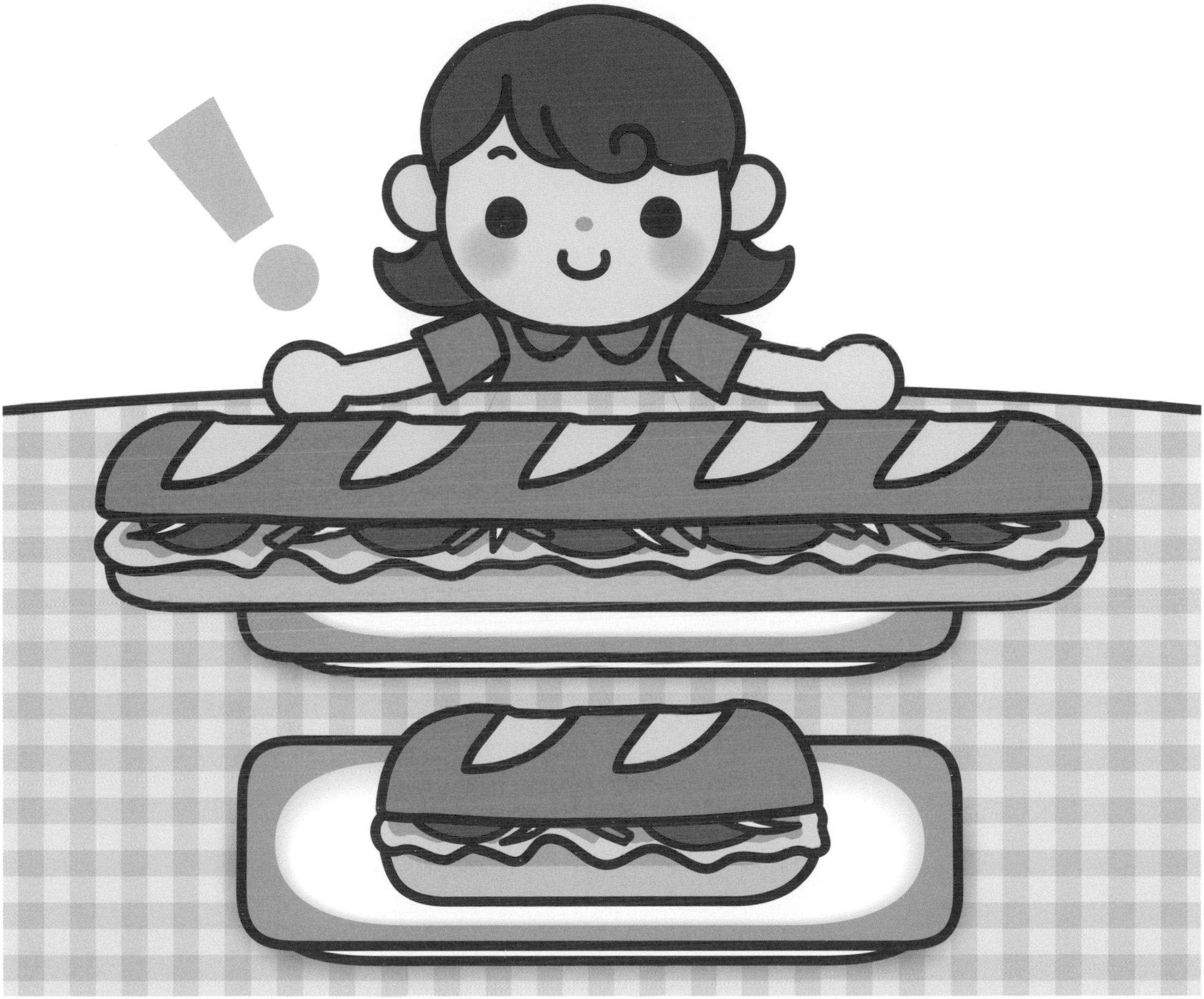

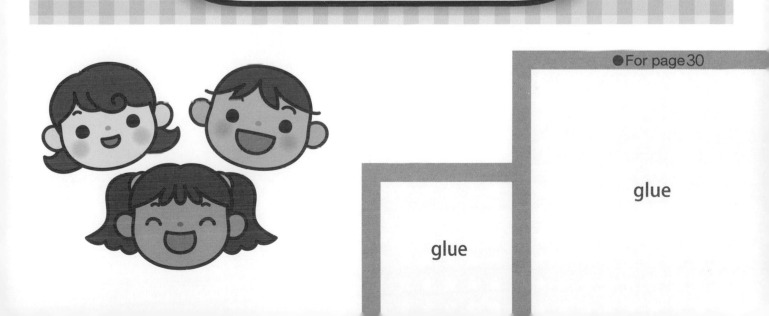

For page 30

glue

glue

Match the Pie to the Box

To Parents: To make sure the apple pie matches the correct box, have your child place the pie piece on the box before gluing it. When done, praise your child by saying, "Well done!"

Which box is the best size to hold each apple pie? Cut out the apple pies and glue them in each box.

paste

paste

Make a Snowman

To Parents: When the activity is complete, let your child color the snowman in their favorite color and draw eyebrows and a mouth. This helps develop their creativity.

Put stickers on the snowman. Color the hat and scarf.

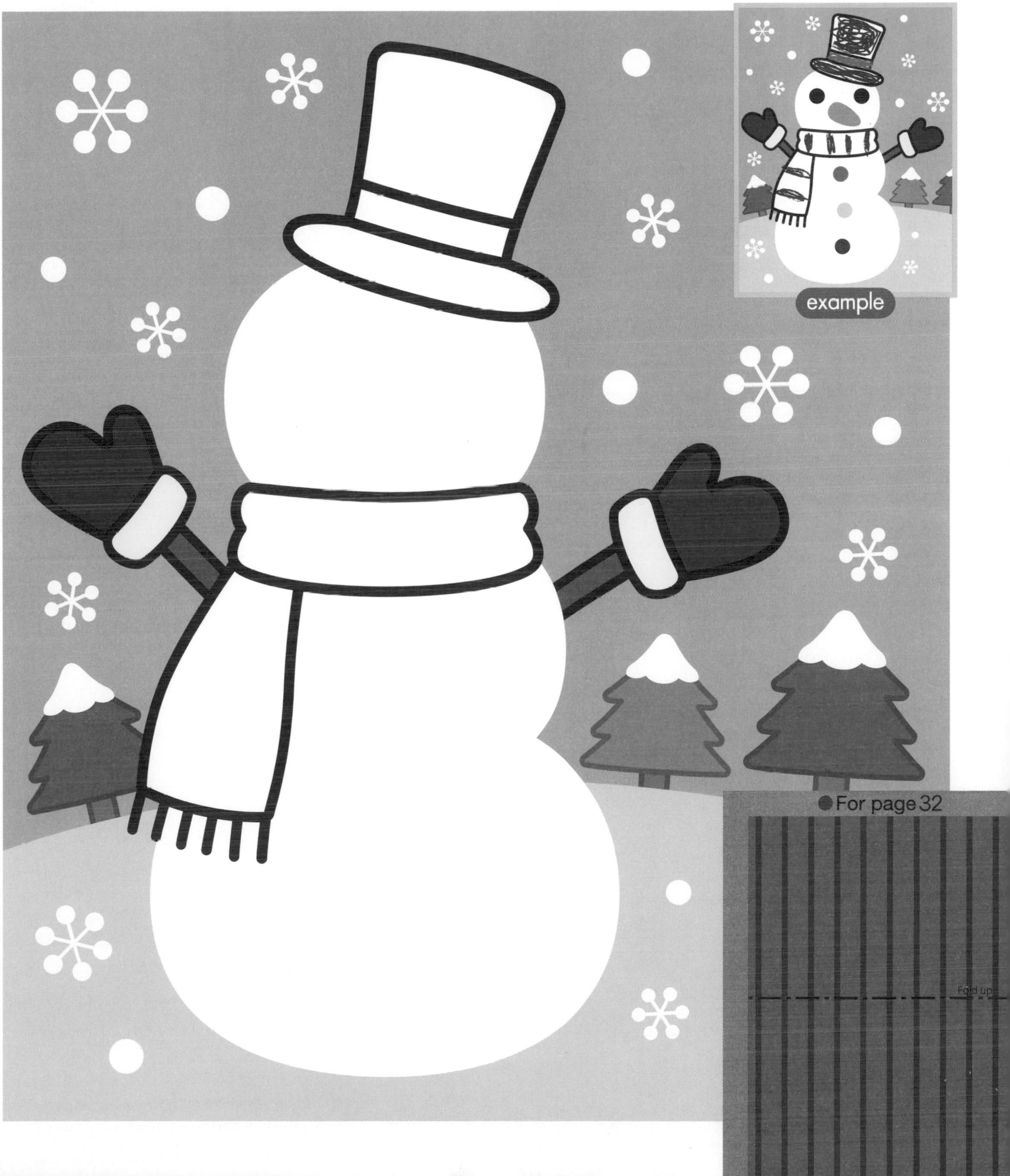

example

For page 32

Fold up

Follow the Path ①

To Parents: In this activity, your child will develop fine motor skills by moving a train along the track. Encourage them to move the train while mimicking its sound.

Run the train along the railroad from  to .

How to Make

Cut out the train.

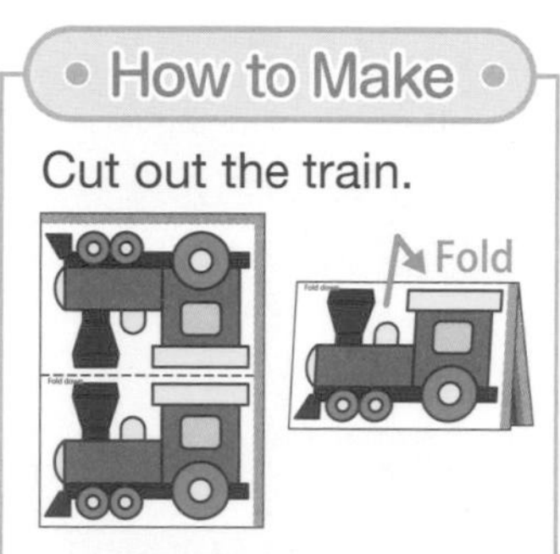

How to Play

Run the train through various paths.

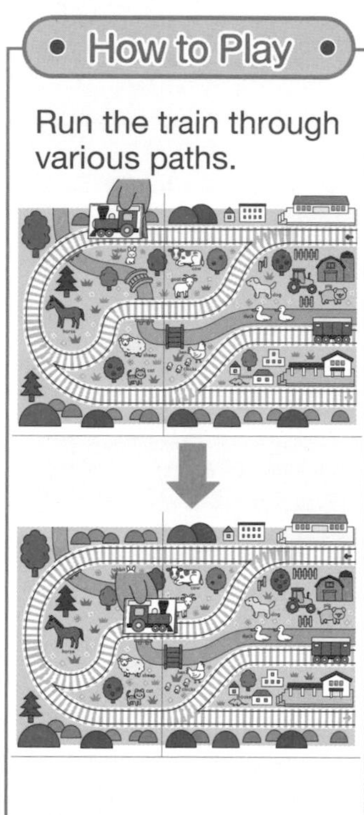

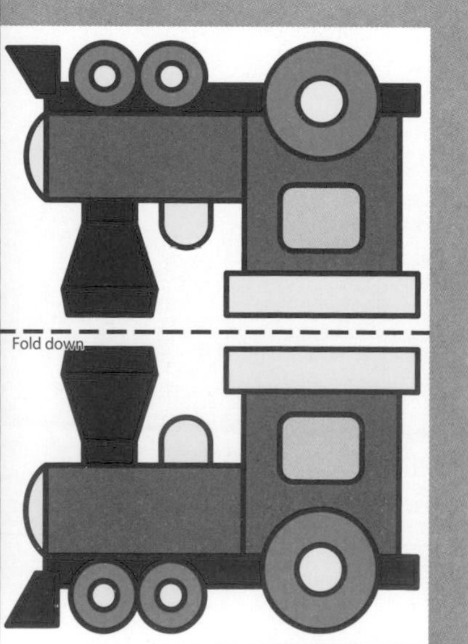

rabbit

horse

sheep

cat

Follow the Path ②

To Parents: Help your child see that there is more than one way to reach the goal. Enjoy the activity while giving further challenges like, "Let's pass by the cat!"

cow

goat

dog

pig

duck

hen

chicks

mouse

Bonus Challenge! Move the train from ➡ to ➡ passing by the goat and sheep.

Trace Spirals

To Parents: In this activity, your child will practice drawing clockwise and counterclockwise spirals. Make sure your child pays attention to the direction of the red and blue arrows.

Trace a line from ➡ to ➡ with your finger.

snail

candy

snake

Bonus Challenge! Trace the lines in the opposite direction.

Complete the Picture

To Parents: If your child is not sure where to put the pieces, ask them to describe what the animals are doing.

Cut out the pieces and glue them on the boxes to complete the picture.

paste

paste

Find the Different Ghost

To Parents: In this activity, your child will practice comparing different objects. If this seems difficult, tell them, "There are ghosts facing different directions."

One ghost is different from the others. Find it and draw a ◯ around it.

Bonus Challenge! Find two red stars in the picture.

Find the Matching Box

To Parents: The boxes below contain similar items. Encourage your child to see the items in the example by saying, "doll, blue car, and red block."

Which box has the same toys as the example? Color the ◯ below the box.

Complete the Picture

To Parents: Encourage your child to look at the examples below and then draw on the face. Your involvement will motivate your child.

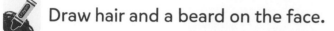

Draw hair and a beard on the face.

example

Picture-Matching Puzzle

To Parents: This activity uses puzzle pieces to build spatial reasoning skills. Pay attention to the shape and picture on each puzzle piece.

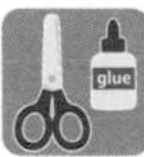

Cut out the pieces and glue them to complete the picture.

paste

paste

paste

Bonus Challenge! Count the number of apples after gluing the pieces.

Make a Fluttering Butterfly

To Parents: After making your butterfly (see instructions on page 41), say to your child, "Stop at the yellow flower next time" and "Move from the red flower to the blue flower." Move the butterfly around your child's head and shoulders. Allow them to do the same to you!

Make a butterfly and let it perch on the red flowers.

glue

glue

glue

Bonus Challenge!

Find three ladybugs in the pictures on pages 40 and 41.

How to Make
paste
paste
Fold
Fold
glue
Cut out a butterfly and a handle.
Fold along the dotted lines.
Glue
Glue
Paste
Paste
How to Play
Hold the handle.
Make the butterfly flutter over the flowers.
Fold down
Fold down
Fold down
paste
Fold up
paste
Fold down
glue

Draw Lines

To Parents: Have your child practice by drawing the curved line on the left first, stopping halfway through and starting again. When they finish, have them draw the curved line on the right.

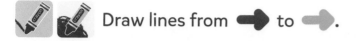

Draw lines from  to →.

Bonus Challenge! Color the sun.

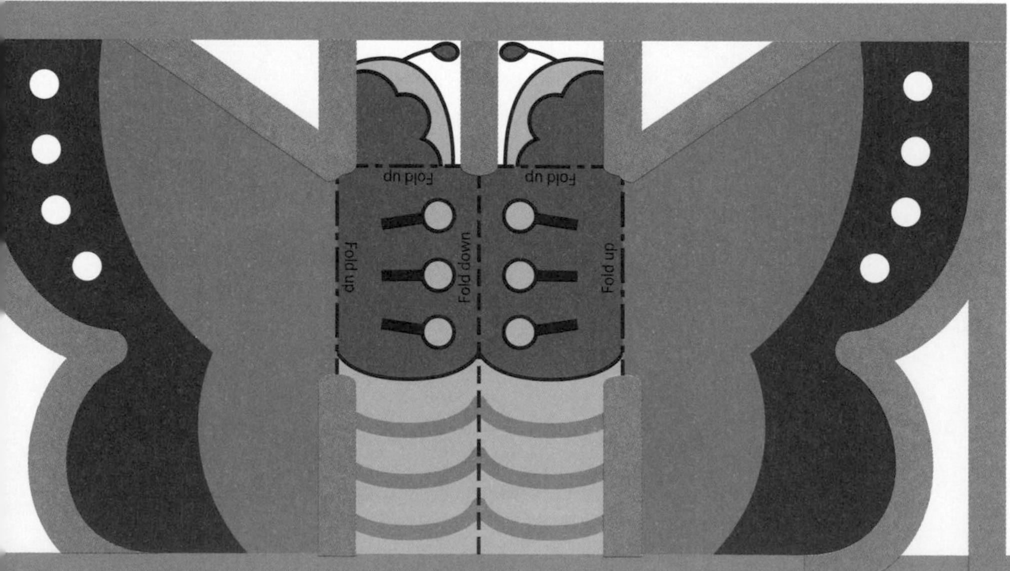

glue

Match the Shadow

To Parents: Ask your child to name the object while looking at the silhouette. If this seems difficult, give them a clue. If they recognize it is the fork, ask them to also find a fork on the right side.

Which object on the right matches the shadow? Find it and draw a ◯ around it.

Go Through the Maze

To Parents: Since there is no guideline from the start to the goal, your child can move freely. If they almost touch the cat, pretend to mimic a cat's paw and reach out to touch the mouse. This allows your child to enjoy the activity while experiencing realism.

Put the mouse sticker on your finger and move it on the path from ➡ to ➡ without touching the cats.

• How to Play •

Bonus Challenge! After tracing, draw a line from ➡ to ➡ without touching the cats.

Move Your Body

To Parents: This activity helps develop gross motor skills by stopping in an instant. Change the timing when saying, "Stop!" If your child gets used to it, switch roles between the two of you.

Follow the instructions to move your body!

Run and Stop Game

Say, "Let's run!" to your child while following them.
Say, "Stop!" to have them stop running.

Swim and Stop Game

Say, "Let's swim!" and pretend to swim with your child. Say, "Stop!" to have them stop swimming.

Guess the Animals ①

To Parents: This activity helps children memorize words that start with letters of the alphabet. After quizzing your child, let them open the picture and say the words themselves.

Follow the instructions to play an alphabet game.

A is for alligator

Fold up

B is for bear

Fold up

C is for cow

Fold up

How to Play ❶

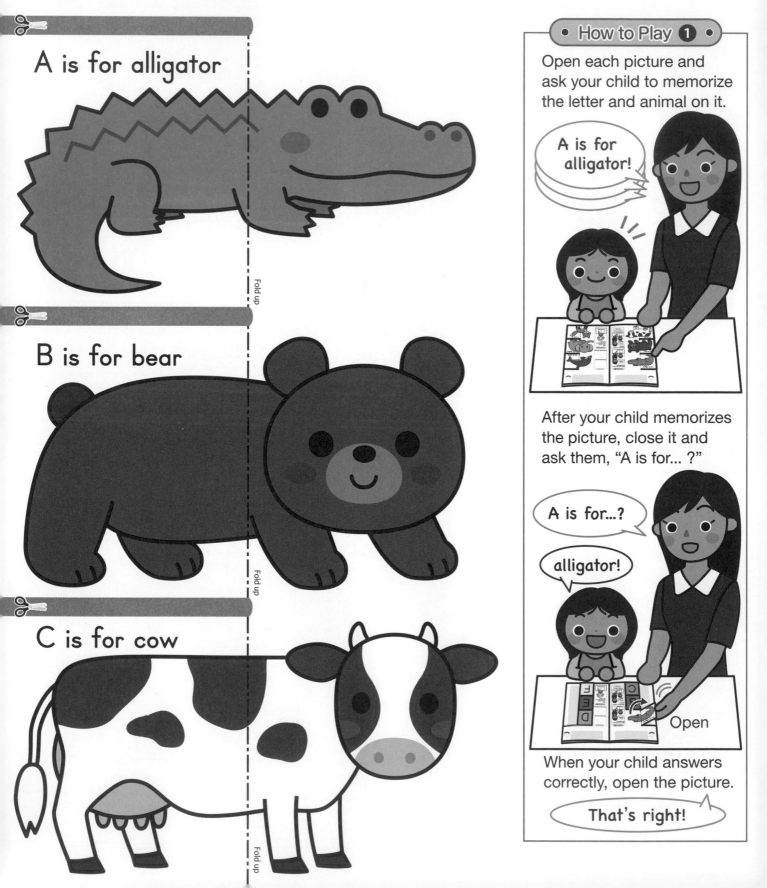

Open each picture and ask your child to memorize the letter and animal on it.

A is for alligator!

After your child memorizes the picture, close it and ask them, "A is for... ?"

A is for...?

alligator!

Open

When your child answers correctly, open the picture.

That's right!

Guess the Animals ②

To Parents: In this animal guessing game, let your child choose from the three options on the side of the page. When done, use both sides of the page to try it with more options.

How to Make

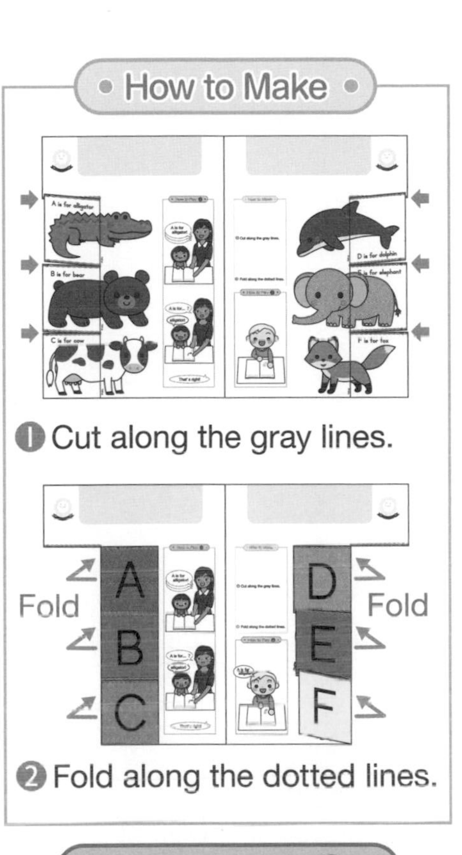

❶ Cut along the gray lines.

❷ Fold along the dotted lines.

How to Play ❷

❶ Ask your child to find the alligator while the picture is closed.

❷ Have them open the picture with the alligator.

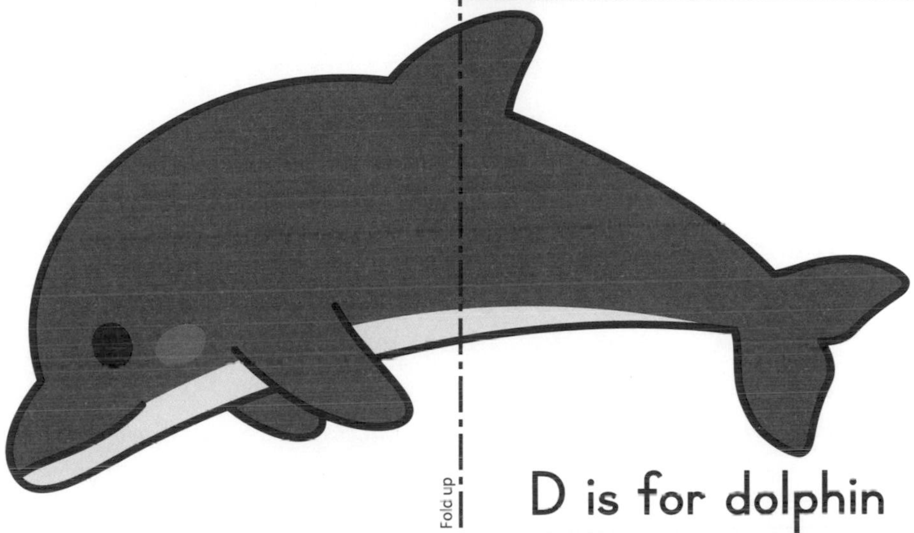

Fold up

D is for dolphin

E is for elephant

Fold up

F is for fox

Fold up

Find the Numbers

To Parents: In this activity, your child will sharpen their observational skills, while spotting hidden objects.

Look at the picture below. Find the hidden numbers 1, 2, 3, 4, and 5. Draw a line to connect each number to its match.

●For page 47

D

Fold down

E

Fold down

F

Fold down

1 2

example

Find the Numbers

To Parents: The style of the numbers might make it difficult for your child to find them. Start by carefully looking for each number in one part of the picture. For example, look at just the merry-go-round.

3 4 5

Bonus Challenge! Trace the numbers one to five in the ☐.

Find the Difference

To Parents: Ask your child to look carefully at each picture. Provide hints for them, if needed. The items that are different in the bottom picture are: sailboat, sun, and bus.

Find the three differences between the two pictures below. Draw a ◯ around each difference in the bottom picture.

Make Vegetable Faces

To Parents: After your child applies the stickers, ask them what kind of facial expressions they made. Then give each vegetable a name, such as "Mr. pumpkin."

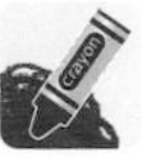

Add eyes and mouth stickers to each vegetable. Then draw hands and feet.

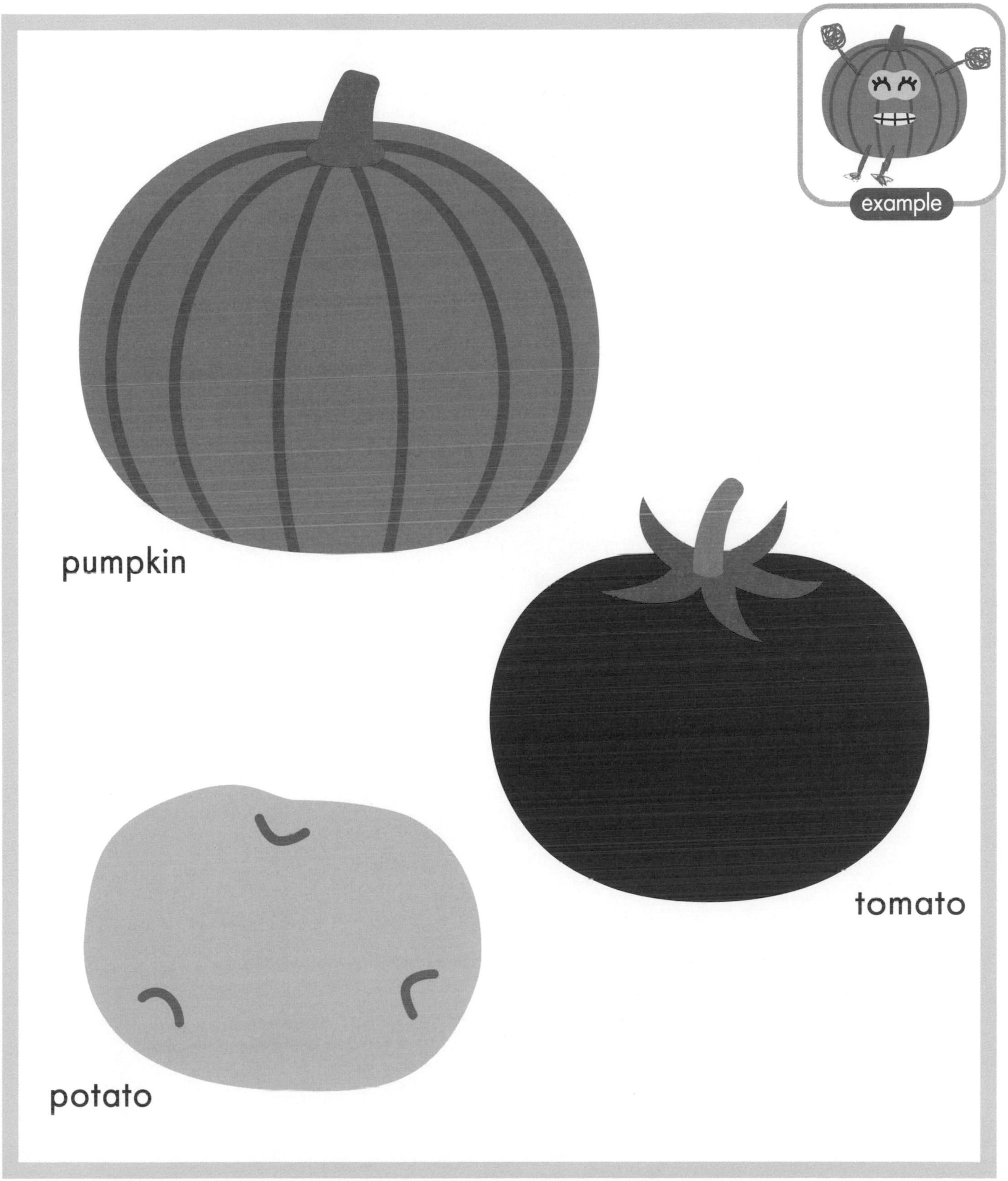

example

pumpkin

tomato

potato

Bonus Challenge! Say the name of each vegetable.

Find the Utensils

To Parents: This activity helps your child develop observation skills. Try giving your child a hint by saying, "There are crabs with different claws."

Find a knife, a spoon, and a fork and draw a ◯ around them.

Bonus Challenge! Find the crab with a starfish!

Draw Lines

To Parents: While closing and opening the paper, say to your child, "One dinosaur, two chicks, and three turtles." And then say to them, "The number of eggs and the number of babies is the same."

Cut the gray lines and fold the dotted lines. Then draw lines from ➡ to ➡. Open each egg and watch the baby be born!

1

Fold up

2

Fold up

3

Fold up

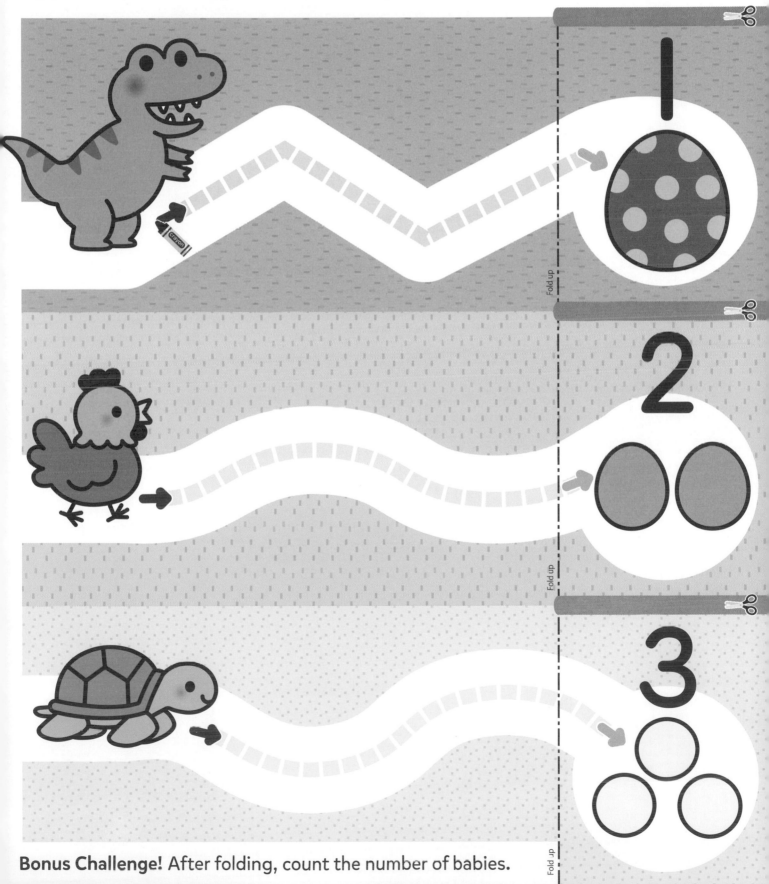

Bonus Challenge! After folding, count the number of babies.

Draw Noodles

To Parents: Encourage your child to draw a continuous line without stopping. Have them use thick crayons or markers to add whatever they want to the noodles on the plate.

 Draw a line from  to . Then draw more noodles on the plate.

Fold down

Fold down

Fold down

Bonus Challenge! Draw meatballs on the pasta.

Spot the Differences

To Parents: Try quizzing your child by asking what is behind the folded paper. Give them clues like, "This animal eats bamboo" or "This animal lives in the water."

Fold along the dotted lines. What animals are hiding?

panda

hippo

How to Play

Fold

Fold up

Fold down

Make Sandwiches

To Parents: Match the size of each plate with the slices of bread and pieces of ham and cheese. If your child is having difficulty, show them the complete picture on page 58.

Make a sandwich and put it on the plate that matches its size.

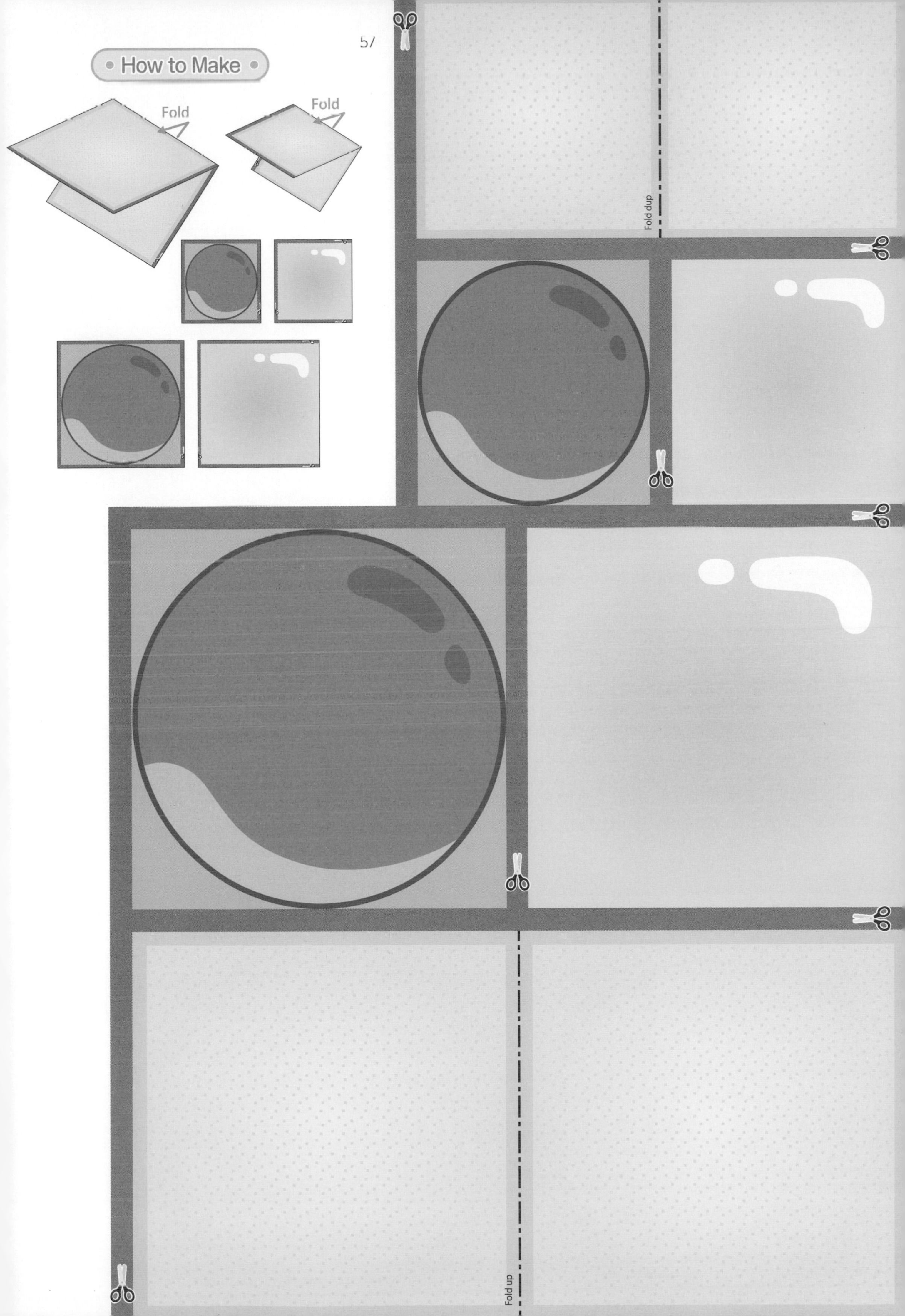
How to Make
Fold
Fold
Fold up
Fold up

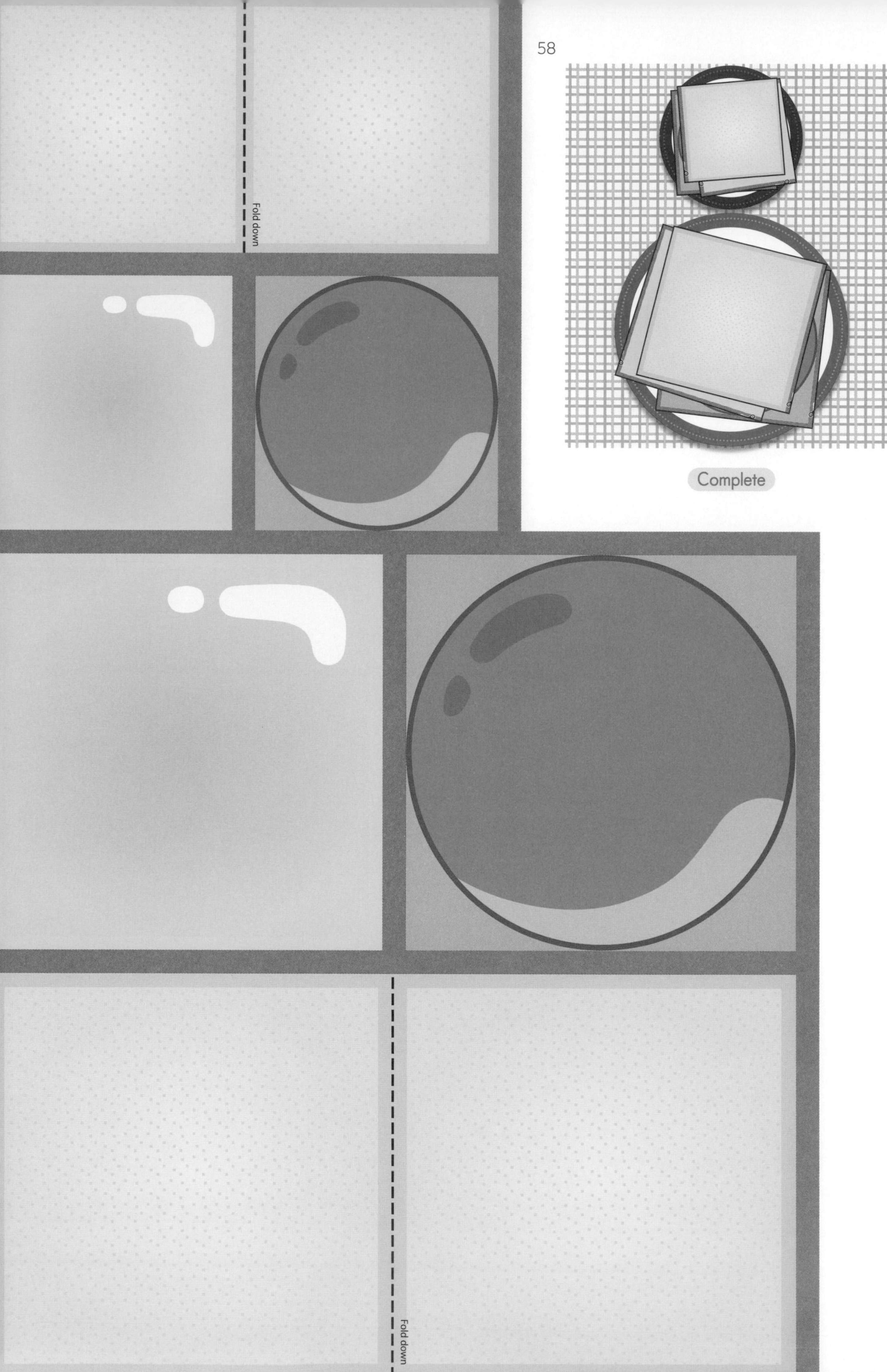

Complete

Place in the Same Order

To Parents: This activity helps your child recognize the positions up, down, right, and left. While pasting, say to your child, "The upper one is a rabbit" and "The lower one is a dog."

Cut out the pieces below and place them in the same order as the example.

example

paste

paste

example

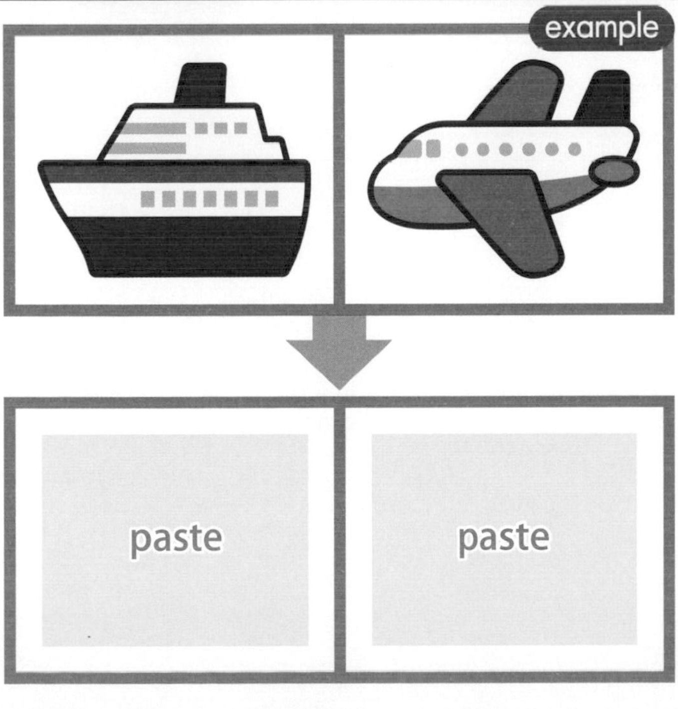

paste

paste

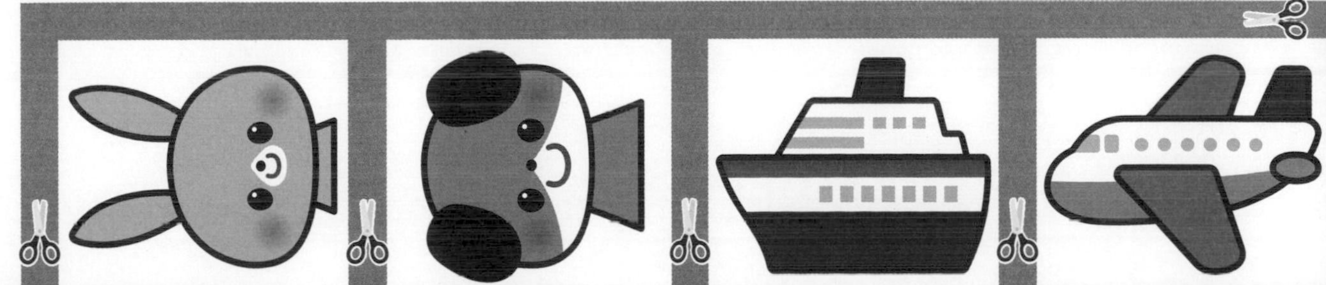

Make a Pattern

To Parents: In this activity, your child must recognize similarities in objects and then put those objects in order according to a pattern or sequence. Have your child say the names of each item out loud (bee, flower, bee, flower).

Follow the path from  to . Put stickers on sticker to complete the pattern.

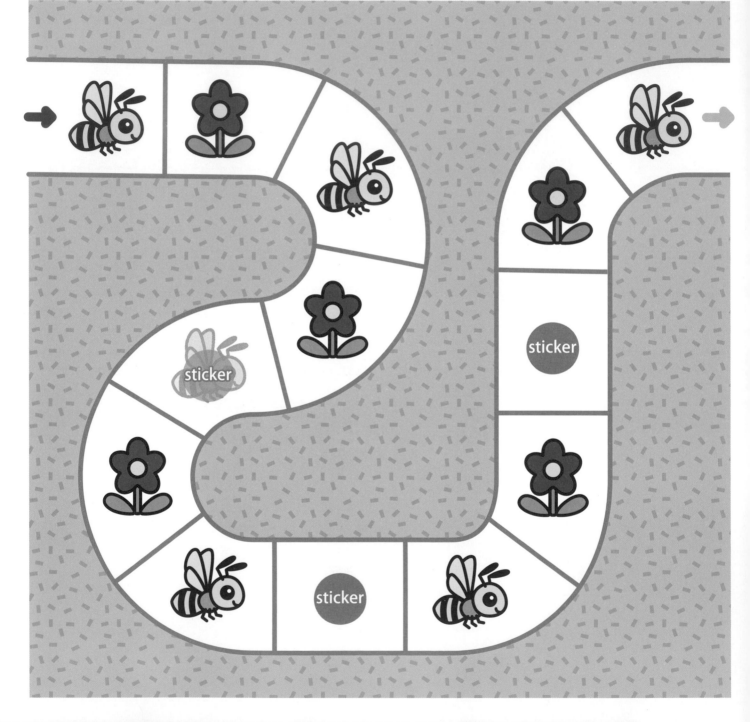

sticker

sticker

sticker

Make a Pattern

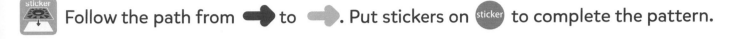

To Parents: Practicing pattern recognition is an important foundational skill in math. After finishing this activity, try familiarizing your child with patterns by pointing out some examples around you (on clothing, toys, etc.).

Follow the path from  to . Put stickers on  to complete the pattern.

For page 62

Build Pictures

To Parents: This activity builds spatial reasoning skills. Have your child place the triangle pieces first and then put them in place.

 Cut out the triangles below and put them on the picture.

Go Through the Maze

To Parents: After drawing a line to the first flower, stop there and then connect lines to the next flower. This will help your child draw longer lines.

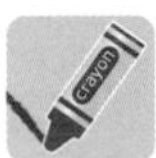

Draw a line from ➡ to ➡ through the flowers.

Bonus Challenge! Count the number of frogs and tadpoles. Which number is more?

Find the Matching Shape

To Parents: If your child is having a hard time with this activity, make an example with an actual piece of folded paper.

If you unfold the paper on the left, what appears? Color the circle below the shape that matches that shape.

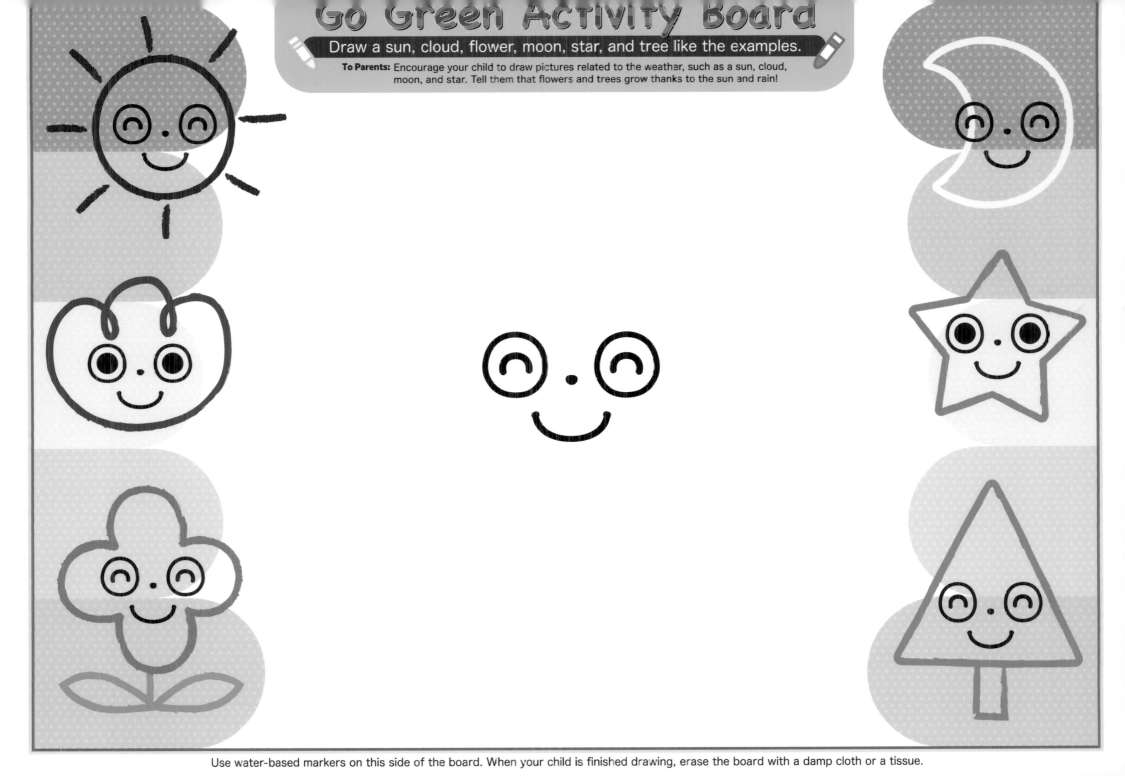

Go Green Activity Board

Draw a sun, cloud, flower, moon, star, and tree like the examples.

To Parents: Encourage your child to draw pictures related to the weather, such as a sun, cloud, moon, and star. Tell them that flowers and trees grow thanks to the sun and rain!

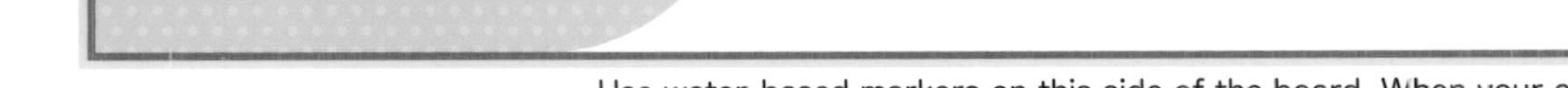

Use water-based markers on this side of the board. When your child is finished drawing, erase the board with a damp cloth or a tissue.

Find the sea creatures in the picture and name them.
Then, find the cup and bottle and circle them.

To Parents: Ask your child what kind of creatures live in the ocean. Tell them, "Many creatures live in the ocean. When we pollute the ocean by dumping garbage into it, these creatures are affected, so we must try to keep our ocean clean and healthy."